MAGIC MIRROR INVESTING

YOUR COMPLETE GUIDE TO REAL ESTATE INVESTMENT

www.MagicMirrorInvesting.com

LARRY YAKIWCZUK   PATRICK NG

Magic Mirror Investing

Your Complete Guide To Real Estate Investment

Buckaru Publishing

www.BuckaruPublishing.com

6 BONUSES

5 Homes to Financial Freedom   FREE
A webinar recording explaining how you can achieve financial freedom with the equivalent cash flow of 80 rentals from owning just 5 homes. (Value of $49.99)
Visit **www.MagicMirrorInvesting.com/book**

Making
FREE
A webinar
ventures and
with very
Visit

Real Money With Joint Ventures

recording discussing the specifics about joint
how they can be a short cut to vast residual profits
little initial work. (Value of $49.99)
www.MagicMirrorInvesting.com/book

Rent To Own with No Money and No Risk   FREE
A webinar recording with over 60 minutes on rent to own secrets and different ways to increase your profits and minimize risks in real estate investing. (Value of $49.99)
Visit **www.MagicMirrorInvesting.com/book**

A Millionaire's Mindset   FREE
A webinar recording giving you an insight into the mindset of a millionaire where you will learn a bit about business, real estate, and the stock market. (Value of $49.99)
Visit **www.MagicMirrorInvesting.com/book**

Power Investing   FREE
A webinar recording giving you an insight into the mindset of a Millionaire where you will learn a bit about the stock market and investing. (Value of $49.99)
Visit **www.MagicMirrorInvesting.com/book**

CONTENTS

INTRODUCTION 1

THE BASICS 3

1 - 11 Myths About Real Estate 5

2 - Where To Find Good Deals 19

3 - How To Analyze A Deal 29

4 - Structuring A Deal And Making An Offer 47

5 - Things To Consider Before Removing Your Conditions 59

6 - Members of Your Success Team 63

ADVANCED TOPICS 73

7 - How To Make Money With Real Estate 75

8 - How To Manage Your Property 85

9 - How To Purchase Property With None of Your Own Money 97

10 - Using Your RRSP To Invest In Real Estate 103

11 - Private Mortgage 105

12 - Renovating Your Property 109

13 - Wholesaling Real Estate 119

14 - What Is Lease Option? 125

15 - Commercial Real Estate 135

ABOUT THE AUTHORS 141

Patrick Ng 143
Larry Yakiwczuk 145

6 BONUSES 151

INTRODUCTION

"Mirror, mirror on the wall, who is the fairest of them all?" asked the queen in the fairy tale. Then the magic mirror would respond to her with an honest answer. In reality, wouldn't it be nice if we all have a magic mirror that can tell us all the answers we want?

For those of us who are interested in real estate investment but lack the knowledge and experience, a magic mirror would be perfect for us every time we have questions. Unfortunately, this mirror doesn't exist in real life. That's why we've created this book to help, inform, and educate you like a magic mirror, and hence, we name our book "The Magic Mirror Investing: Your Complete Guide To Real Estate Investment."

In this book, we'll discuss all the elements in real estate investment at two different levels. At the basic level, you'll learn about the fundamental knowledge for buying real estate. First, you need to separate the truths from the myths so that you have a clear understanding of the subject before you start to jump onto the boat. Then, we'll show you the process in a step-by-step order, such as where you can find deals, how to analyze deals, how to make an offer and finally how to close the deal. Of course, it's unlikely that you can succeed in this business all by yourself. That's why we'll also explain to you who you should partner up with.

In the advanced topics, we'll show you more complicated concepts in real estate investment as you're ready to take your investment to the next level. For instance, if buying a property isn't easy for a novice investor, renovating and managing one is definitely even more challenging. We'll tell you what you can do to facilitate your property renovation and management and to protect yourself. Then, we'll explain the different ways real estate can earn you profits (i.e. profit centers), how you can sell a purchase contract instead of the underlying property (i.e. wholesaling), and how to profit while helping people in a "rent-to-own" arrangement (i.e. lease option). And the most interesting topic of all, we'll show you how you can invest in real estate without your own money!

As you can see, real estate investment is more than just buy-and-hold; there are a lot more strategies available. But of course, more options also come with more potential for pitfalls. So, after finishing the book, you'll have the knowledge to devise an investment pathway that suits your own needs and preferences.

THE BASICS

CHAPTER 1

11 MYTHS ABOUT REAL ESTATE

When you start investing in real estate as a beginner, you will hear different options and advice from many people around you. But how do you know which ones are trustworthy, and which ones are misleading?

One of the things you should always ask someone giving you advice is what their experience is. Have they actually done investment before or are they just reciting propaganda and being an arm chair quarterback? The old saying that comes to mind is "Those who cannot do, they teach." To decide for yourself if we truly know what we are discussing, please read the "About the Author" pages later in this book.

In order to make informed decisions with real estate investment, you need to differentiate truths from myths. Here are some of the myths that you need to take heed, and the real truth behind them.

MYTH # 1: REAL ESTATE IS A SHORT CUT TO BECOMING RICH

Despite the major global financial crises, when you look at the housing market throughout recent history, the price trend has been either skyrocketing or has been able to quickly and tremendously recover from a market correction. In fact, you may even have friends in your circle who have already made a fortune in real estate. So it's tempting for you to think that you can make big money quickly with real estate investment. This makes you feel you need to jump into the real estate game quickly, or else you'll miss out.

Indeed, some real estate investors do make lots of money quickly, but essentially what they're doing is house-flipping, or what we call real estate speculation, not real estate investing. Those people are basically risk takers who play very risky speculation games based on short-term market conditions and trends, and get lucky with their gaming. They are neither truly educated, nor have any specialized real estate knowledge and make irrational decisions with economics fundamentals in mind.

But of course, you can also make money in real estate without taking any risky actions. There are many low risk methods, but they require your patience and a long-term horizon; you need to start building your wealth with one property at a time, and grow slowly and steadily over time. Real estate is NOT a get rich quick scheme; it is a get rich slow system. And that's the principle behind this book.

MYTH # 2: INVESTING IN REAL ESTATE IS VERY RISKY

While some people are eager to get their hands on real estate, you have others at the opposite end of spectrum who stay away from real estate. They want to avoid it at all cost because they think it's too risky.

What they fail to realize is that their fear and avoidance actually come from their observation of investors who have the wrong mentality, the wrong strategies, and have lost money by speculating with real estate based on the wrong market trend. So, if you only focus on property appreciation and hope to make quick buck by doing a flip, then you're making real estate investment risky.

Now let's compare real estate with other types of investment and put risk in perspective.

In our opinion, investing with term deposits and other guaranteed investments is a risky move. Your average term deposit will only bring a tiny percent of return per year (e.g. 0.5% to 1%). When inflation is currently going at 2% to 3% a year, you are actually losing ground by using these products as an investment. By using those financial vehicles, you're at risk of losing money in a paradoxical way.

When you put your savings in mutual funds, not only will their values go down along with the stock market, they also have mandatory management fees. Does this potential downside make mutual funds any safer than real estate? By law, mutual funds have to stay fully invested in the products mentioned in their prospectus, even if the market is falling. They cannot go to a cash position in order to prevent losses. So in reality the mutual fund is designed to absorb losses of the stock market. Also, remember that most mutual fund fees are actually hidden, and include things like front loads, back loads, management expense ratios, account fees and so on. It has been estimated that your total fees on mutual funds can be as much as 6% to 9% a year. That means that your mutual fund has to make 6% to 9% just for you to break even! Not to mention that most financial advisors are nothing more than high priced commission sales people, who ONLY make money when they convince you to buy or sell something!

When you put your money in stock market and watch it tank by 5% to 20% in one single trading day, this kind of volatility is far riskier than real estate. If you look at the overall markets over the last number of years, they generally are at about the same level that they were at. There have been highs and lows, but overall no movement. Your profit or loss is determined whether you exit on a high or a low.

Personally, we would much rather have slow, consistent increases like what you get with long term real estate investments. This is the type of investment we personally specialize.

MYTH # 3: YOU HAVE TO BE WEALTHY TO INVEST IN REAL ESTATE

This is one of the biggest misconceptions that beginner investors have! When you think about purchasing a property, one of the first few considerations that come to mind should be the down payment because you know that, without some money from you as a guarantee, nobody will have faith to lend you the huge remaining portion required for the purchase. And if you already realize that you cannot come up with a down payment, you may feel as if you'll never have hopes in touching the real estate sector.

In reality, what you really need is access of money. While one way of access it is from your own pocket, who says you can't have access of money from other people's pockets? That's right, you can start investing with other people's money! And here is another bonus for you: many people think it's impossible to have deals with no-money-down. But it is possible! Of course you can't do these kinds of deals with the traditional banks. That's why you seek other options like private financing.

There are many ways to do no-money-down deals. For example, you can use other people's (i.e. investors') money as down payment, and then get a mortgage from a bank. The bank doesn't really care whose money the down payment belongs too, as long as you have one. As long as you have cash in hand you have fulfilled their deposit requirement.

Another way is to use your own line of credit for down payment. You may argue that line of credit is not truly no-money-down because you'll have to repay it eventually. But technically, that's still not your money; that's the bank's money lending it to you for a down payment. Also, you may not even have to repay the line of credit out of your own pocket because, later, you may have other investors jumping onto your boat, or have rent from your tenants to cover it.

Even if you're completely broke or, worse, in debt, you can still invest in real estate. As long as you can demonstrate to others your sound knowledge and strategies in the area, and show them why it's worthwhile and beneficial to invest with you, you will always be able to find capital from them for the down payment you need.

If you lack the time, energy, knowledge, or motivation to invest in real estate, or you are just too hesitant to invest in it yourself, you can still do it. This is what we specialize in. We partner with people who have some money to invest in real estate but do not want to do it themselves. They can invest with us as an investor and have their investment secured by the real estate we purchase. They do none of the work, receive above average returns, and have their investment secured by real estate.

MYTH # 4: THE BANK IS YOUR ONLY OPTION FOR FINANCING

This is another big misconception that novice investors have. Traditionally, you think you need to go to a bank for a mortgage or loan because other options, like mortgage brokers, cost more money and are not as reliable. But the truth is, you don't necessarily need the bank. When you deal with a bank, you're working with just one lender, and this narrows down your choices of financing. Alternatively, if you do your research well and choose a good mortgage broker, not only do you have the option of top 5 banks, you'll also have access to many different lenders from all across Canada. What's more, you don't even need to pay for your mortgage broker's services. With any new residential mortgage businesses the brokers can generate, the banks (or the lending companies they partner with) will pay for the broker's commissions.

Essentially, you don't need to deal with your bank at all. Once you get a good mortgage broker who can find you the best deal, you'll then have the financing you need at a good price. Later on we will discuss how a mortgage broker can be a very valuable asset to your investment team.

Private financing is another alternative. Rather than using a bank or lending institution for the bulk of the money needed for a real estate purchase, you use money from either an individual or group of individuals. Their loan to you is recorded as a mortgage against the property. In essence these individuals are becoming the bank for you. This is a very good investment for them as they get fixed rates of return over long periods of time and their investment is fully secured by the property. Although it is not well known, this can also be done with RRSP money.

We routinely use private money and RRSP funds to generate mortgages on our properties. If you are an investor with funds ready to go, and don't want to do any work related to real estate investing but still want the consistent returns, please contact us directly as we ALWAYS have investment opportunities available.

MYTH # 5: YOU HAVE TO USE A REALTOR WHEN YOU BUY REAL ESTATE

No, you don't! You might think, as an inexperienced investor, you must use realtors in doing deals because they know more about real estate than you do. This myth is perpetuated mostly by realtors themselves. In most cases, realtors have limited training for what they do and they may not be best qualified to do every type of deal. Also, with potential conflicts of interest, they aren't always the best person to represent you in every deal. Not to mention there are some bad, unethical agents in the bunch who only care about transactions and commissions, so you must do your research to find a good one for you. To some extent, realtors could be helpful to you, especially at the beginning of your investment journey, but you don't absolutely need them to do a deal. In a later chapter in the book, we'll talk about how to choose a good realtor and make them part of your success team.

Alternatively, you can choose to work directly with the sellers because there are definitely advantages to having such direct relationship. For instance, direct dealing with sellers gives you more control during negotiation, so that the process, price and contract terms can be determined the way you want it. But with a realtor, you'll have to pass your offer through one or more intermediary before it can reach the seller. This may lead to miscommunication & distortion of your intended ideas and requests, thereby losing control of the negotiations.

MYTH # 6: IF YOU USE A REALTOR, YOU CANNOT TALK TO THE SELLER DIRECTLY

Another myth perpetuated mostly be realtors is that you can't contact the seller directly (they will say it's not legal or not permissible). Your realtor or the listing agent is not going to be too keen on linking you up with the seller, as they fear that they would lose a potential sale and, hence, their commissions once you bypass them. So you have to let them know ahead of time that their assistance is still valuable to you.

You actually have the legal right to present yourself to the seller, either in person, or in a letter attached to the offer saying who you are & what you want. You can request your realtor or the listing agent to establish a direct contact between you and the seller. It's important for you to try to reach the seller in some way so that you can gain some control in the negotiating process. If you can deal with the seller directly, you can then ask the realtor to write up the contact for your deal.

A good agent will always allow you to talk directly to the seller, and also negotiate directly with them. If you are good at presenting the deal to the seller, that means there is less work for the agent to do!

MYTH # 7: YOU NEED TO BE A SLUMLORD TO PROFIT IN THE REAL ESTATE BUSINESS

Not necessarily! Indeed, there are all sorts of dishonest or unethical businessmen and landlords out there who would prey on other citizens, seniors, or poor families to make profits. Those are the greedy people who like to rip people off by offering the least while trying to get the most out of it. But you don't need to become such in order to make money. If you put yourself into their shoes, you should strive to provide your tenants what they legitimately pay for, such as clean and affordable housing – the same level of housing you would want to live in yourself. You as a landlord with integrity can still make money by building or maintaining open and trustworthy relationships with your clients.

The simple concept we use when dealing with people in the real estate industry is to treat people the way we would like to be treated. Look for the win-win scenarios and offer to help people who have a problem.

There is a way of thinking that the more people you can help, the richer you will become. We are firm believers in that strategy.

MYTH # 8: EVERYONE IS OUT TO TAKE ADVANTAGE OF ME

As we have just stated there are slumlords out there that will try to take advantage of you. However, we are big believers in the idea that you will find what you are looking for. If you believe that everyone out there is trying to take advantage of you, then you will naturally be drawn to those types of people and you will see them everywhere. If you believe that people are generally good natured and willing to help you, then you will naturally be drawn to those types of people.

This myth is actually a corollary to the previous myth, and the same concepts apply. When dealing with people in the real estate industry, treat people the way you would like to be treated. Look for the win-win scenarios and offer to help people who have a problem. Remember the more people you can help, the richer you will become!

MYTH # 9: DEALING WITH TENANTS IS A NIGHTMARE

In reality, how you deal with tenants is a choice and will only be a nightmare if you let it become that. Everyone has heard those horror stories of being woken up in the middle of the night to a screaming tenant saying their toilet is broken and overflowing. If that happens to you, all that means is that you are an inexperienced property manager and do not have the proper systems in place to deal with unpredictable emergencies. Property management is an important aspect of real estate investment, and we devote a full chapter to this later on in the book. In fact, there are full courses on just property management.

The simple solution for the plugged toilets is that you have a simple clause in your leases and rental agreement that states that the tenant is solely responsible for plugged toilets and sinks, and it is their responsibility to deal with them. It is also a good idea to have a pre-arranged deal set up with a plumber, and to provide the tenant with that plumber's contact number as part of their welcome package you give them at the start of their tenancy.

Remember that your tenants are arguably the most important component in your real estate investing. They pay your mortgage, they pay your expenses, and they give you your profits. So if you treat your tenants fairly and with respect, they will eventually make you very wealthy.

MYTH # 10: YOU WILL NEVER FIND A GOOD DEAL IN REAL ESTATE

Why do you make this assumption? No matter what the market condition is, good deals always exist. Good deals just come up more frequently in a buyer's market than in a seller's market. You'll be surprised to find out that some sellers will sell their properties at significant discounts anywhere from 10% to even 50% below the current market price. Those properties are in deep discount because of some unusual or unforeseen circumstances, such as a change in people's lives. Often, sellers may be going through divorce or sudden layoff that forces them to relocate and sell their places quickly. In some cases, the properties are so poorly managed or even neglected to a point that they require expensive and labour intensive repairs.

Remember when making an offer, cash is king, and if someone is desperate for cash, they may be willing to significantly discount their assets just to get some fast cash, especially if they are under some form of time pressure such as foreclosure.

MYTH # 11: THERE ARE NO DEALS ON MLS (Multiple Listing Service)

Many people think that because the MLS is open to everyone, they could never find a good deal there. Nothing can be further from the truth. There are many reasons why you can find deals on the MLS.

Stale listings are a good source of deals. These are listings that have been on the MLS for a long period of time, and have been seen by everyone, and no one has completed the deal. After a while the vendors will be getting very desperate just too even get a showing of their property. The agent is no longer interested in promoting the property because they perceive it as a waste of their time, so there is probably a deal to be had here.

If the property has a problem of some sort and it is listed on MLS, most potential purchasers really do not want to deal with problems, and the property will routinely get passed over.

We actually found one of our best deals as a stale MLS listing that had some problems. It was some land that was going through a foreclosure and judicial sale. It had been listed on the MLS forever, and no one wanted to deal with the red tape needed to close. The property was listed for $450,000 and we eventually purchased it for $405,000. That is a full 10% under list. You may think, "Big deal, it is only 10%!" But after we purchased it, we had it appraised for a total of $600,000. That means we bought this property for over a 30% discount, while it was listed on MLS!

CHAPTER 2

WHERE TO FIND GOOD DEALS

There are a few considerations before you head out and start hunting for deals. First, you need to know what you want to gain from real estate investment. Once you have a clear vision of your practical and financial goals as to where you want to go and what you want to achieve, you can then decide the composition of your real estate portfolio that is best for you. For instance, you may prefer more proportion of condos in your portfolio since you dislike maintenance by yourself. Also, you may like the sense of community or security that condominium complexes offer in a particular neighbourhood. But most likely it is because condos are the cheapest way to enter the real estate market. It's very important to have your choices fit your vision.

Next, you need to identify the characteristics of your interest areas. If you're investing in your home base, chances are you already have a pretty good idea of various parts and people of the city. But what if you want to invest in areas outside of your familiar zones or even in a different city? Well, you can drive around town with a map. Pay attention to the types of local businesses that serve that neighbourhood; they'll give you clues in the kind of residence and demographics in the area. In places where you cannot see or manage the property yourself, you would first need to find a property management company in which its services are up to your satisfaction and it operates in your target city. Make sure you have someone in place to look after your property before you start hunting for a property.

After knowing the place you want to invest, you then visit your real estate agent and ask for help in looking for your desired type of property in that area.

WHAT CAN I INVEST IN?

Several types of investment properties are available and suitable for new investors: single family homes, condominium, townhouse, and multi-units properties like duplex, triplex and quadplex. You also have more complex options like entire apartment buildings, but those should be reserved until you have more experience in deals and property management.

As a starter, you may not be able to do deals right away. That's why it's a good idea to stay focused and educated, so that you can learn to become an expert in identifying deals. Even if you spend months just tracking property sales in your interest neighbourhood, it's still a good learning experience for you to find out the true value of properties in that area. All the time you spend in training yourself would allow you to recognize and jump on good deals quickly when opportunities eventually present themselves.

Regardless of the type of property you want to purchase, you need to realize equally both the pros and cons that come with it. You could be blindsided by enormous expenses and liabilities in the future if you focus too much on the pros at the time of decision-making. Since each type of property has different advantages and disadvantages, let's examine each one of them and see which one(s) fits your vision and preference.

Condominiums are the favourite type of property investments for the beginner. Condos are most likely to be the least expensive option among all types of property. Less maintenance is definitely a huge bonus for condo ownership. After you purchase a condo unit, you only have to maintain the inside of your unit; the outside structure of the whole building will be taken care of by the condo board collectively. But this benefit comes with a significant problem, especially if you haven't done your homework properly before your purchase. If the condo board has insufficient or even non-existing reserve fund set aside for big capital repairs like roofing or siding, the board will approach each unit owners for an enormous cash call when the time comes. If you can't cough up the money, they have the right to take your unit back. So practically, you pay for only the inside of a unit, and when you can't fulfill your duties for the entire building, your control over your condo will be severely limited. Also, a monthly condo fee is another nuisance that is out of your control. Keep in mind that if you're thinking about buying a brand new condo, the developer may set the condo fee for the first few years low & manageable just to lure you in, but then the fee may skyrocket and your expected cash flow could disappear in a flash. So you must do your due diligence beforehand and have a lawyer with some experience in condo to help you prior to your purchase.

Detached single-family homes are also a common type of investment property for beginners. With this type of property, you're responsible for handling everything yourself, which may require a lot of time, labour, and management skills. But unlike condominium where there is a board that imposes rules & regulations on you, you get to set your own rules and schedules on how your investment business should operate.

Semi-detached homes like duplexes share a portion of the common areas. From developer's perspective, it's cost-effective to build this type of property because they can put more units on less space. From your perspective as a landlord or investor, while the sale prices of semi-detached homes can be lower than those of single-family detached houses, the much closer proximity of your unit to your neighbour can create a potential problem. Regardless of what or who initiates the dispute, when you get a tenant in your place that doesn't get along with the neighbour next door, you'll have a headache managing your property and the interpersonal relationships among all the parties involved.

Larger residential complexes are also a very good investment vehicle. These deals tend to be a little more complicated and definitely beyond the beginner level. However, after you have done a few simple deals, we would definitely recommend you gradually deal with these larger complexes.

We routinely invest in larger residential complexes such as condo complexes, apartment buildings, and even commercial properties. If you do not have much real estate investment experience but still want to get involved with these larger deals, we are always looking for financial investors to partner with us on larger deals we are considering.

PROSPECING FOR DEALS BY YOURSELF

Once you identified the kind of property and location you want, it is time to start looking for a prospective investment. Getting help from others such as realtors or other investors is definitely beneficial, but don't forget to do your own due diligence by actively marketing yourself and searching for deals. You can start with "for sale by owners" properties, also known as FSBO's.

The primary reason that a FSBO homeowner sells their house by themselves and not by a listing agent is that they want to skip the agents' commission and save money. But without the input of experienced realtors, they often don't know how to assess their property values properly. That's why a lot of those properties may be over-priced or under-priced. When you've done your homework well, you have an edge over those owners who don't have knowledge of the market or the required negotiation skills. Your advantage will then allow you to negotiate for and make some good deals.

If you happen to come across houses that are over-priced, you don't have to bargain vigorously and try hard to close the deal right away.

Sometimes, pushing too hard may actually yield the opposite result. You can always leave the option open by thanking the homeowners politely for their time, and leaving your name and phone number in case they change their minds in the future. You'll then move on to your next home on your list. Alternatively, you may make a low ball offer on the spot to test the water. If they have already tried to sell their homes unsuccessfully for the past few months and they're now eager to sell, they may work with you.

One of the most important skills to be learned in negotiation is active listening. When you listen actively and ask the right questions, you can figure out the pains of the seller. And if you're able to come up with a solution that can address the pain and build a trusted relationship, you have a higher chance to reach a deal. Thus, active listening is the critical first step.

From our experience, we learned that keeping the initial pricing reasonable and realistic is crucial because you want to catch buyers when your property is still fresh and hot in the market. Let's say a house is listed for $450,000, but you estimate it to be worth only $425,000. So you approach the seller and offer to buy it for $400,000. Most likely the seller will refuse the offer, unless they're desperate. While the refusal is understandable, the seller may fail to realize that many serious buyers will actively look at the property within the first few weeks of listing. But if it's still available after that time, the seller will have more difficulty selling it, even when he/she drops the price 3 months later. By that time, the seller may reconsider your original offer of $400,000. Since pricing will impact the timing and bargaining power of property sale, correct pricing is very important.

Oftentimes, new investors will get very excited about the new opportunities in real estate investment and are eager to make deals when they first start out. But that excitement (emotion) causes them to pay too much for their first house. That's why it's not a good idea to buy the first one they see. Instead, look at a few homes at the very least before you make your first deal. Although not set in stone, the general rule of thumb is, you analyze at least 100 properties, make offers on at least 20 of them, and then maybe buy 1 or 2 of them at the end. This process might sound tedious, but it gives you experience to assess deals more objectively and get you your first deal at a good price.

We call the process of looking for FSBO deals and opportunities by yourself 'prospecting.' Just like in gold mining, you first have to prospect for a good location, and when you find it, you start mining for your profits. In order to prospect for those private listings, you can check the classified ads on local newspapers, internet (e.g. Comfree, Kijiji, and Craigslist), or drive around your target location. Sometimes you might even see a house that's not advertised in any ad but it has a 'for sale' sign on the front yard.

When you start to talk with a seller, it's very important to ask them if their properties are currently listed with any realtors because technically they can't deal with you when they are committed to realtors' agreements. If a seller is already working with an agent, he/she would either need to cancel the MLS listing with the agent, or to wait until the agreement expires, or else you have to make the deal through the agent.

Besides seeking deals, part of the 'prospecting' process requires you to create exposure of your investment business in the eyes of the public. You'll need to put out a lot of ads in newspapers and websites, and street signs in your target area saying that you have an investor looking for properties. Why do you do that? Preferably, you want to have people call you instead of the other way around, since those callers are potentially motivated sellers and interested in making a deal, which makes your negotiations easier. It's nice to have them chase after you while you're comfortably in control. Many people who first see your ad may not be interested in selling their properties at the time. However, when the time comes, your ads have already left them an impression so they can contact you. We have lost count of how many times we have been contacted by a seller from some advertising material that we had distributed over six months prior to their contacting us. And of course, be sure to make those ads attractive and run them on a regular basis.

When you look at a FSBO home, it is important to tell whether it's a rental property or not. Look for features like neglected and messy lawns, broken windows or doors, or even garbage in front yard, etc. If the house is in a decent neighbourhood but looks like it's suffering from a bad tenant, you might have just found a diamond in the rough and a potential deal for you to pursue.

HAVING OTHER PEOPLE PROSPECT FOR YOU

Once you identified the kind of property and location you want, it is probably a good idea to get help from a good realtor. He or she can't be just any realtor; that person must specialize in the type of property you're interested in, so that he/she will be able to provide you with in-depth information that is relevant to your case.

How can you find such a real estate specialist? A good start point is to look at local listings on newspapers and internet. The realtor with the most listings of your desire type of property is obviously a good initial contact.

A good agent is valuable in the beginning stage of your real estate investment journey because he/she may have access to deals from various ways, such as published listings on MLS (Multiple Listing Service), the hidden ones that aren't yet listed on MLS, and/or private listings through his/her own network in the field. In a later chapter we will explain why having a Realtor on your success team is a good idea.

As important and helpful as a good realtor is, he/she shouldn't be your only source of information; you can go through the MLS website yourself to search for your own deals, just in case your realtor misses something. In Canada, the website is www.realtor.ca, and you can google similar databases for your own country.

Another good resource for finding deals is from networking, like a real estate investor club. It may seem contrary for you to try hunting for deals in a place where everyone else is also hunting for deals. But the truth is, not every investor is finding the same type of property or scale of investment as you are, so there are ways of helping each other out for mutual benefits. Let's say you discover a good deal in a 4-plex but that's not really your interest. In that case, you can still put the property under a contract, and then offer it to other members in the club. Once someone is interested in your offer (or contract), you then assign it to him/her and make a small profit out of it. This is technically called wholesaling, and we have a whole chapter on it later in this book. Similarly, other investors in the club may come across deals and will do the same thing, so you may be able to grab a decent deal from them through this assignment process. Many of these investment clubs actually have whole websites devoted to listing available deals that their members have found and are now available for transfer to other members.

We routinely pick up deals from other people and other investors. If, after reading this book, you come across a deal that you think is good or want to become a part of, please forward it to us, as we routinely give out finder's fees to clients for bringing us new deals that we complete.

CHAPTER 3

HOW TO ANALYZE A DEAL

By now you've realized real estate investment is possible for everyone – even with no money for down payment – and you have learned where and how you can locate deals. So you've decided to jump into the real estate game. You already know which neighbourhood you're interested in and what kind of properties you want to invest. You've also been looking through a lot of deals, and a few of them are really attractive that catch your attention. But now you face a problem: how do you know which deal is potentially the best one for you to pursue? How can you tell if a property will stuff your wallet fat with cash, or suck your wallet dry in the future? In this chapter, we'll show you how to analyze a deal to determine the quality of investment property.

YOU CAN'T ALWAYS TRUST THE SELLERS

The first lesson in analysis you need to know is about the sellers. Why? Because they're the homeowners who know about their properties the most and you'll need their firsthand information to be accurate and reliable so that you can make an informed decision. However, even though most sellers are honest, with their self-interest to sell the properties, be aware that they may not tell you the entire truth all the time. For example, in order to boost the saleability of the property, a seller may understate the incurring expenses and/or overstate the generated income from the property so it looks more attractive to potential buyers. Does it mean that you shouldn't trust all sellers and don't bother looking for deals? Not necessarily. You can get over the hurdle by assuming that all figures and information are for reference only; what the sellers give you may be incorrect – especially if the numbers look really, really good and not realistic – so you do your own due diligence. It's best to keep the mentality that there is something wrong with the seller's numbers but the deal is worth checking out regardless.

DETERMINING YOUR POTENTIAL INCOME AND EXPENSES

The next step in deal analysis is to check out some numbers to see if the property is going to be a money maker or money looser. This is when you have to consider the two important components: income and expenses. Income is any revenue that the property can generate, which can include rent, parking or garage rental income, and signage rental. However, with your first investment property most likely being a single family home or condo, your revenue will most likely come from rent alone.

Income

If the house you're interested in is currently a rental property, it'll be easier to figure out the rental income because you can ask the seller to get a rough idea. But with a home that is occupied by a homeowner who isn't paying rent, you'll have to do some market research to find out what the comparable rental income will be if you were to rent it out. Either way, this type of market research should be done as part of the analysis to determine the property's value. How to do research for the rental market? You can check with the newspapers and internet (e.g. Kijiji, Craiglist) to see what similar properties in that neighbourhood are renting for. And to make sure the rent estimate of your property is reasonable in the rental market, you should also look at market rents for all different types of houses, such as condos, 2- & 3-bedroom homes, townhouses, bungalows, and 2- & 3-stories, etc. One thing to keep in mind is what the rent comprises in your target area. Does it usually include utilities (power, heating, water and sewer), telephone and internet, yard maintenance, or any other type of expense? This is important to know for keeping the rent competitive in the rental market.

Another good idea to see if your rental estimate is accurate is to spend a few dollars and place a local rental ad in your local newspaper, or post a free ad online. If you do not get any replies, then you are either overpriced or there is no demand for the type of accommodation. If you are flooded with replies, then you have underestimated the demand and price, and that's a good sign!

General Expenses

Once you have an idea of income potential of the property, you'll then need to estimate the expenses that the property will incur so that you can get a big picture of how well income and expenses are balanced. The most common expenses include power, heating, water and waste, property taxes, home insurance, mortgage, and yard maintenance and repairs. If you own a single-family home, you have the option of passing many routine expenses (e.g. power, heating, water, yard maintenance) directly onto your tenant on a monthly basis. But with those annual big expenses (e.g. property taxes, insurance, mortgage), you'll have to amortize them and have your tenant cover them through monthly rent.

Now that you've learned the importance of income and expenses in deal analysis, but as a starter investor, where do you get those numbers in the first place? One way is to ask the seller and/or listing agent. But as we said before, they may not tell you the whole truth. For example, if they give you the potential rent figure as opposed to the actual one, you may not make as much income as you expect. Even if, at the end of a calendar year, they show you the actual expenses for that year, those figures are accurate but probably won't be the same next year due to various factors, such as an increase in property tax and utility costs. At the end, that will require you to adjust your forecast accordingly. That's why you shouldn't be 100% dependent on the information from the seller and/or listing agent.

In case those numbers are provided for you, you need to do your own research or verification once you have locked the property under the contract. You can ask them for expense receipts, such as property tax receipt, utility bills, and insurance bills. Alternatively, you can contact your own insurance agent to get a quote for home insurance.

Also realize the possibility that some sellers don't even know all the expenses they may have for their properties. For example, they may have been doing their own advertising, repairs and maintenance all along, but they've never allowed for costs for themselves, or have simply forgotten about them. So you need to thoroughly ask and include all related costs in order to determine the property's true value more accurately.

Once you get their most recent expense numbers, there are a few more factors you need to consider before you can estimate your own numbers for this (and future) years. For example, the insurance for a homeowner who owns a single-family residence and uses it as his/her primary residence will definitely be less than the insurance you would pay because the house is insured as homeowner occupied. Your insurance amount can potentially increase as high as 50% when you turn the same house into an investment property. Check with your own insurance company for a more accurate estimate.

Property Taxes

For property tax, you may have to pay more than the current homeowner, even though you know exactly how much his/her tax payment was last year. That's because when you buy the property, you will trigger a new property tax assessment, which is calculated based on new assessed value. So the owner's number won't be your number. Let's say the owner shows you the property tax of the house being assessed at $250,000 last year. But when you buy it this year at the current market price of $300,000, the new assessed value is going to be in a range close to this price, and hence, your tax could instantly go up by 17%. Since the assessment

process varies among different cities and jurisdictions, your best bet would be to visit your local tax office or city authorities in your target area to find out the current tax rate & mill rate; mill rate is a number the city applies to the assessed value of the property to come up with tax figure. Once you have the two numbers, you can calculate the property tax.

Regular Maintenance

Then you have regular maintenance, which is an expense that many sellers often overlook. You as a landlord have legal obligations to maintain your property by fixing/repairing anything that is broken. If the water tap is leaking, you'll need to fix it. If the furnace isn't producing heat in winter time, you'll need to call up a certified technician to look at it immediately. If any of the appliances you supply for the tenant isn't functioning, you're responsible for repairing that too. Maintenance is a huge and costly duty of owning properties, so it would be a smart move if you don't supply any appliances, thereby cutting actual/potential maintenance costs, such as not supplying appliance. For things that you can't get away from, make sure you factor them into your expense estimation. Of course, maintenance doesn't mean you have to go clean your property regularly (e.g. toilet, walls, lawn); it's your tenant's job to keep your property in decent shape.

Property Management Expense

Wait, you have more expenses coming! For property management, you either need to pay someone to take care of your house and tenant, or to pay yourself or allow for that expense if you're doing all the work. With general maintenance, bookkeeping, and advertising, you can absorb those expenses by doing them yourself, but don't forget to recognize those are the costs associated with the property. You need to include these expenses in your analysis of the property because you can be sure the mortgage company will want to see them in your numbers!

Capital Cost Expenses

Besides regular maintenance, you will also have some potential or actual annual maintenance, or capital cost maintenance. Those are the big, expensive items like furnace, hot water tank, roofing, and concrete patio. From our personal experience, when you initially go through inspection on the property to determine what it needs to be fixed, the paramount action on your inspection list should be having the furnace inspected by a furnace technician. If it already has a problem, the seller would need to fix it before your purchase, or you may agree to get it repaired yourself, with the condition of a sale price reduction of the property by the seller.

It's true that it isn't always easy to estimate future maintenance expenses; it involves a lot of guess work. For example, you need to estimate how much longer the existing furnace can last, and how much money you'll need to reserve for a new replacement in case it blows up unexpectedly or when it reaches its anticipated end of functional life. You can either make an educational guess, or get professional opinion from a certified technician.

Once you know what you expect to repair/replace in certain number of years (e.g. 3 years) and figure out a certain amount you need for the fixing, you should start saving money on an annual basis so that, in the end, you'll have enough money for those expenses. For condominiums you generally do not have to worry about this, since the condo corporation is responsible for the major repairs to the property. Just because you do not do it does not mean it is not done. In reality it is taken care of by what is called a reserve fund study, and that is used to determine your condo fees within the complex.

Conclusion

The general rule of thumb is, your expenses should never exceed 40% of your income. And it would be even better if you can get the percentage lower. So let's say your rental income is $2000/month, and then your expenses should be less than $800/month, excluding your mortgage payment. And it's preferred that you can get your expenses as low as possible. After all your expenses and mortgage are paid, any remaining money would become your profit (or cash flow). As an investor, you need to expect certain level of cash flow from your investment property. Although different investors have different levels of projected cash flow, the bottom line is, you shouldn't invest in any property that can't generate net positive cash flow.

INCORPORATE A REALISTIC VACANCY RATE

When you use income and expenses to calculate net operating income, or NOI, you're assuming your property is fully occupied. But question yourself, "How well do my numbers work out if my house isn't 100% occupied all the time?" That's why, in order to think more conservatively to weather worse scenario, you should consider vacancy rate as well. In fact, when you go to the bank, your lender will assess your financing qualification with the rate included. So while the current homeowner may tell you that he/she never has any vacancy, which may be the case, you should still include the rate. You can visit Canada Housing & Mortgage Corporation website to look for the vacancy rate for the neighbourhood of your interest. Here is how you use vacancy rate in your calculation:

Gross Operating Income - (Vacancy Rate x Gross Operating Income)

= Effective Gross Operating Income

Effective gross operating income is the figure you should rely on when you operate your property. If it turns out to have no vacancy, then think of it as a bonus for yourself. But you should never overlook the possibility of vacancy. There are a few vacancy-generated expenses you should think about as well, and marketing is one of them. If your investment unit sits empty without generating any income, you'll need to advertise it to get a new tenant. You don't need to spend thousands of dollars on newspapers; even a few hundred dollars in advertising costs will go a long way, especially with the options of free advertisement we have nowadays, like internet (e.g. Facebook, Craigslist, Kijiji), and local community bulletin boards at laundromats and grocery stores. One of the most cost effective & productive advertising methods is to put up a sign on the front yard on your property or in the front window. Sometimes you may get 40% to 50% response on that sign alone. So it's a good idea to invest in a custom-made sign, which looks more unique and professional than those you can buy at your local Home Depot store. Another vacancy-related cost is cleaning after a tenant leaves. This falls under maintenance section, which will be discussed later in management chapter.

SET A REALISTIC EXPECTATION FOR YOUR CASH FLOW

In the previous section, we brought up the concept of cash flow and emphasized its importance. But how exactly is it calculated? Here's how we get the cash flow value:

All income from property (effective gross operating income)

–   All expenses for property (not including the mortgage)

Net operating income (NOI) before debt servicing

Net operating income (NOI)

–   financing cost (e.g. mortgage)

Cash flow (profit)

During your deal analysis, you should consider your minimum cash flow – the minimum amount of profit you're hoping to gain from this investment after all the endeavours. But you need to be realistic in setting that goal; if you're aiming to gain a cash flow of $500/month for each individual rental household, you'll probably be frustrated with not getting what you want. From personal experience, a target profit of $50 per rental household per month seems reasonable. So if you rent your single family house as 2 households (main floor, and then a basement suit), then you'll have $100 a month. If you have a 10-unit property with one household in each, then you'll get $500. When you can get more than $50/month, good for you, but that target is the absolute minimum that you should set.

COMPARE WITH OTHER PROPERTIES IN THE AREA

Not only is the value of your investment property determined by how well it can generate income (or cash flow), it's also influenced by comparables – the prices of other comparable houses in your target neighbourhood. To avoid over-paying for your deal, you should find out the actual worth of the property by comparing its asking price with the recent transactions (within the past 6 months) of other homes in the same area that were similar in style, age, and conditions. Let's say other houses in that area were all sold for about $300,000, but the deal is asking for $325,000. Then you'll have to ask yourself, "What feature(s) of the property justifies the extra $25,000, or am I simply over-paying for this deal?" Once you've paid attention to and researched a neighbourhood of your interest for a period of time, you'll have a pretty good idea of what the property value is actually worth. If you don't understand how to do the research or haven't had enough data from your own research, you can ask your realtor to help dig out some comparables for you. He/she has access to the MLS system with the behind-the-scene numbers, such as how much that property has been sold for in the past few years. It'll only take them a few minutes to pull up, for example, 10 comparables in the neighbourhood of that property which have been sold in the last year. That information will be very helpful in assessing whether or not the purchase price is reasonable.

HOME VALUE APPRECIATION FOR YOUR TARGET AREA

The housing market trend also plays an important factor in your deal analysis. Is the price of property in your neighbourhood of interest, going to, stay flat, rise merely by 1% to 2%, or skyrocket like in Vancouver or Toronto? This is an important question because, obviously, you want to invest in an up and coming neighbourhood that has potential to grow in the future. That way, the housing prices won't go anywhere but up. One way to forecast the growth potential (and home value appreciation) is to try to find out the municipal plan for the existing and future development of that neighbourhood. For instance, is there a good transit station already established, or will there be public transit system extended to your location any time soon? Is there any new industry or industry expansion in your town (e.g. IT development)? Any planned business closures that you can foresee (e.g. oil and gas industry downsized due to dropping in commodity prices)? Are they planning on opening a dump in that empty field across the street? How about municipal government marketing plan for the town growth (e.g. tourism promotion)? Those are all essential questions that can help you determine how much potential and appreciation your neighbourhood will have.

ONE TIME AND CLOSING COST EXPENSES

You also need to consider some one-time expenses that you'll have to pay upfront at the closing of the property purchase.

Generally, most financing institutions and lenders require you to submit a loan application fee of some sort. Most institutions will just subtract this fee from the mortgage proceeds they give you after the loan is approved. If a private lender or broker requires you to submit large sums upfront as an application fee, you should be skeptical of them, as there is no guarantee that you will be approved by the lender, and it may be just some scam to get cash from unsuspecting novices. Depending upon where you get your financing, you may have an appraisal fee. Sometimes the bank or lender will incorporate this into their loan application fees.

When you hire your lawyer to prepare and go through legal documents for you, you'll definitely need to pay for legal fees, which you can ask your lawyer ahead of time.

Home inspection is another must-do in property purchase, and that expense is unavoidable. In fact, you should budget for two inspections – one for checking the house, and another one specifically for roofing.

Then you have other expenses that are region-dependent. For example, in BC and Ontario, you have provincial land transfer tax. Even worse, in Toronto, you have two land transfer taxes! Always ask your lawyer in the area of your property purchase because he/she can help you identify those costs, so you wouldn't be surprised down the road.

FINANCING THAT FITS YOUR SITUATION

Your own finances will determine how you can fund a deal. For your property of interest, how much can you afford out of your own pocket for down payment? And then how much will you have to ask from the bank or broker as a loan? Undoubtedly, the more money you put down, the less money you repay the bank, the less your mortgage expense, and the more positive your cash flow. But the trade-off here is, the less money you borrow from the bank, the more you have to use your own cash. So leverage and profit are inversely related. You need to weigh the pros & cons of different options to see which one will fit your need and confidence level the best. Let's say you have two options: 50% from bank & 50% from you (50/50), and 80% financing & 20% your own money (80/20). Obviously, with 80/20, your cash flow will go down as your monthly mortgage payment is higher, but you probably feel okay with that arrangement because that can free up more of your cash to buy a few more properties than just one. Maybe that's what you want to do, who knows? If you are a fist time home buyer, you may be able to get even higher mortgage financing up to 90% or 95%.

Whatever options you have in mind, discuss with a knowledgeable mortgage broker. He/she can explain to you how different financing composition has its pros and cons, and how different interest rates and terms impact your long-term real estate investment vision and strategy. For instance, if you're planning to hold on to the property, or when the interest rate is very low, you may want to think about lock-in terms and fixed rates. If you're planning to keep the property for just a short time and flip it in near future, you may want to consider a variable rate mortgage that is fully open for prepayment at any time.

PROPERTY ANALYZER

Dealing with so many variables in your deal analysis can be overwhelming, and sometimes you may forget to include some expenses here and there. That's why a property analyzer, which is like a pre-set spreadsheet, is highly recommended. With an analyzer, it'll allow you to collect your data in an organized manner and avoid overlooking any expenses, even the less obvious ones. Plus, it can highlight certain crucial information. Another big benefit of an analyzer is the ability for you to play around with the numbers so that you can visualize different scenarios with various inputs. You can play with adjustments using the traditional pen, paper and calculator too, but it'll be a lot more cumbersome.

There are many different property analyzers out there. A good one should be simple or intuitive to use. Otherwise, you'll become overwhelmed by it. Remember, an analyzer is supposed to facilitate your analysis process, not to hinder it any further. And keep in mind that, it's definitely a helpful tool, but it's not a replacement of your knowledge, common sense and intuition; you still need to keep up-to-date with your real estate investment learning, so that you know what to look for, what questions to ask, and how to determine true property value and cash flows.

A good idea is to use an analyzer that is recommended to you by another successful investor. You do not need to spend a lot for a property analyzer. You can find many free analyzers on the internet. If you have even a basic knowledge of excel you can even program your own spreadsheet to calculate anything you want to.

NECESSARY OBJECTIVITY

During your analysis of the deal and property, you must keep a cool head to make a logical judgement and not to get emotionally attached to the property. Ask yourself questions like, is the house located in the neighbourhood I like to invest in? Does the property fit your financing qualification and needs? Does it have lots of repairs now and even more expenses down the road that will blow out my budget? Will it generate enough cash flow to meet my expectations? I know it's difficult to think logical sometimes, as you may fall deeply in love with certain feature of house like its big, open kitchen. But try to treat the property just like an income generator, not object of affection, so you won't buy a lemon.

Oftentimes, you need a second opinion with your decision-making. So it's important to have an experienced real estate agent to help you, especially one who knows about rental property. Never let fear of making mistakes stop you from trying and learning. We have made a lot of mistakes and errors in our investing career. It has been an expensive learning curve that we do not recommend. That's why you should start simple and small with one single-family home or condo as your first investment property. You can manage and overcome any mistakes more easily at a smaller level than if you invest in a 30-unit apartment building. As with everything else, the only way to become better at what you do (real estate investing in this case) is to take action and start the process and then to learn from your mistakes.

If you are completely paralyzed when it comes to real estate investing, remember that you can always just become a cash investor and partner up with someone who is far more experienced than you. That way you can achieve a decent return on your money and learn at the same time. We are always looking for cash partners to invest with us on various projects. Please contact us for current opportunities.

CHAPTER 4

STRUCTURING A DEAL AND
MAKING AN OFFER

After you analyze a deal and believe it's a good investment property, you decide to purchase it. But how do you make an offer, and what items should you include in it?

As a consumer in daily life, we are used to paying for everything, like clothing and grocery, in the full amount according to the price tag. But in real estate, you never pay the listing price; you need to negotiate instead. After your analysis of a house goes well, the first thing you should determine for the deal is the maximum price you're prepared to pay. Of course you're not going to offer that price to the seller; that's just a price ceiling that you stick to. Basically, it helps set a parameter for negotiation so you can go in with a low offer and feel more confident in bargaining with the seller. Beware that your offer doesn't go too low because the seller might find you insincere or even insulting to him/her. He/she may then simply walk out of the negotiation, and you'll lose your chance to build a relationship

and iron out a deal. So your offer should be realistic but at the same time lower than what you're willing to pay. Never start your negotiation with your maximum price in mind (i.e. last card); you'll have no more room to bargain afterwards.

When both parties agree on the price, you then need to draft up a purchase and sale agreement. It can be as simple as writing names and prices on a piece of paper. But at least for your first deal, I would strongly recommend you to get a realtor to draft you the paperwork, making it legal & binding, because the process and regulations may vary from area to area. For example, you may know thoroughly how to buy real estate in your home area, but the rules in another jurisdiction might be slightly different, and you don't want to put yourself in a blind spot right in your very first deal.

A GOOD AGENT CAN HELP YOU A LOT

You might have been working solo throughout a big part of the process, like doing research and negotiating deals all by yourself. But in making the offer, it's definitely a smart move for you to bring in a professional real estate agent. In this important stage, you do want to lay out all prices and conditions clearly and legally on documents, so that you won't be paying for any hidden expenses or accepting any surprises later, which will cost you more than what you will pay when bringing in a realtor.

How should you compensate the agent for creating a legal and binding offer? You can do that through a contract setup called seller's or buyer's commission. In the contract, you have the option of setting up with either a set percentage or a flat fee. For percentage commission, it's typically 3% to 4% of purchase price, but could be as low as 2%. And for a flat fee, $1000 to $1500 for the service seems reasonable. In fact, the fee-based commission is preferred because, after all, the only thing the agent is really doing for you is legal paperwork.

Once you hire an agent, you'll ask him/her to go through the whole process with you, such as collecting legal information (e.g. names, addresses of both parties and land title) and explaining what standard fixture is and isn't commonly included in the sale (e.g. water tank, furnace, central air-conditioning, or home appliances if you request).

It's very important to remember that, in your offer to buy a property, you should specify on document the items you're asking for. For example, if you fall in love with the stainless steel fridge and stove in the kitchen and you want to include those in the deal, you should specifically write that you want that particular stainless steel fridge and stove to remain in the kitchen. With model brands and numbers on paper, the writing can ensure that you won't end up with an old fridge and stove, when the owner takes away all your desired appliances with them when they move out.

Alternatively, you can take pictures of everything in the house while you're doing the viewing. Before doing so, you should ask the homeowner for permission to take some pictures and explain that it's for your own reference to avoid any dispute later. If he/she replaces the appliances before you take over the property, you can show the photos and say those are what you bought under the purchasing agreement.

PROTECT YOURSELF BY USING ESCAPE CLAUSES

As you can see from the above example, when you buy a property, you can't finish the transaction right away with signing some legal documents and transferring payments; you need to make sure you'll get exactly what you set out to get with no surprises. That's why you first make an offer to the seller. Essentially, an offer creates an option for you to buy through a purchase & sale agreement upon meeting various conditions.

There are a few conditions that you can set in the offer using the "subject to" clauses. In the next few sections we will look at some of these clauses.

Subject To Satisfactory Financing

As much as you want to buy a property, you can't always guarantee you can get the money for it, unless you pay in full with your own cash. That's why you put a condition for financing in your offer. Some might suggest you to speak with your mortgage broker or banker for a pre-qualified mortgage prior to hunting for any deals or making any offer, in which, for a single-family property, it's reasonable for you to visit your lender about two weeks beforehand. While you can do that to guarantee funding and save you time in the process, that shouldn't save you from making the offer subject to financing because the property itself needs to be assessed. When you visit the bank, not only will the lender check to see if and how much you're qualified for a loan, he/she will also see if the house's condition is qualified for a loan. In case the seller's information is incorrect, the bank may turn you down and you'll still end up with no funding. Or you might change your mind and decide to renegotiate the deal with better terms. Either way, the financing clause gives you an escape door so you're not legally stuck in a deal you can't or don't want to move forward. Using the word 'satisfactory' is very important in this clause because it can also give you a way out of a sticky situation. Sometimes, banks will offer you financing but with unsatisfactory terms that you really cannot live with, or if the banks are not interested, the seller may offer you his/her own financing. Technically, you now have found some financing, and a seller or realtor can argue that the condition has been satisfied. But because you use the term 'satisfactory' in the clause, you still have a way out if the financing offered is NOT satisfactory to you.

Subject To Satisfactory Inspections

When it comes to inspections, it's highly recommended that you don't have just one inspection but multiple inspections. Different inspectors will check different parts of the home, such as structure, furnace, and roof, etc. This can ensure the condition of each specific part of the property is as good as described by the seller. If a problem is discovered during the inspection, you'll then have the option to either renegotiate the deal, or walk away from it. Without this clause, you'll lose any options to work things out before settling the deal. Again, using the word 'satisfactory' is very important in this case because it can give you a way out of an undesirable situation. Sometimes, inspections will come up with problems that you really don't want to fix or too big/complicated for you to handle. At that moment, you technically have had the inspection done, and the seller or realtor can argue that the condition has been satisfied and force you to close the deal. But because you use the term 'satisfactory' in the clause, you can still say the outcomes of the completed inspection is NOT satisfactory to you, and walk out from the deal without further obligations.

Subject To Seller Providing At Least One Year's Worth of Bills

As we said before, sellers' expense information may not always be correct, so you should verify the accuracy of all those numbers by looking at the actual bills.

You need to ask the seller for at least one years' worth of expenses from the property. These should include power, water, heating, insurance, taxes, and anything else that may be relevant. However, with home insurance, you can look at current owner's receipt for comparison, but you should contact your own insurance agent to find out how much your insurance will be, since different insurance company and homeowner's background will generate different insurance rate. And for property tax, you need to contact your local tax office or municipal authorities for more information on what property tax rate you can expect after you buy the property.

If the seller claims to not have the utility bills, you can always contact the utility companies directly and obtain copies from them.

Subject To Satisfactory Inspection of Current Lease

If the house is currently a rental property, you can look at the lease to verify that the rent, as described by seller, is indeed true. Confirm that the rent is paid monthly and punctually, and the amount stated isn't deceitfully inflated. Verify the remaining duration of the lease and that legitimacy of lease itself. It would be even better if you're able to find out if the tenant is happy and in good standing, so you know what kind of tenant you'll be dealing with once you take over the property. Again, using the word 'satisfactory' is very important here. Sometimes, leases may have some terms and conditions in them that are outrageous, and you simply cannot accept them. Now that you have technically inspected the lease just by reading it, the seller or realtor can argue that the condition has been satisfied. But since you use the term 'satisfactory' in the clause, you still have a way out if the lease terms are NOT satisfactory to you.

Subject To Lawyer's Approval

Once you present your offer to your real estate attorney, he/she will check it objectively for anything tricky or possible mistakes to ensure your protection. For whatever reason, if you want to bail at this point, this clause will give you a good chance to do so without further obligation. Keep in mind that this clause will only be effective for a few days after the contract has been created. Not only does it provide time for your lawyer to examine the structure and detail of the deal, it's also a good cooling period for you to really consider your intention to purchase. At this stage, your lawyer isn't digging into the property history yet because he/she usually checks that 2 to 3 weeks before closing.

Subject To Partners Approval

This is a very generic escape clause that is also a very good negotiating tactic. You can use it to get out of a deal if you decide it is no longer attractive to you, or you can use it to negotiate some changes. As example, you can say, "My partner is very pleased with the deal but wants new appliances. Is that something you can install to close the deal?"

Everyone has a partner, whether it is your spouse, your financial partner, your pet, or just your legal advisor. You can always use your partner to your advantage.

THINGS BESIDES THE CLAUSES

All the above clauses are usually included in the main agreement or as an extra attachment called 'Schedule A' and placed with the main purchase and sale agreement. While the actual agreement will contain legal information such as names of buyer and seller, land title, property address, and any home accessories included or excluded, Schedule A includes anything else you may want to include. Within the agreement, pay attention to something called the 'irrevocability date' or 'acceptance date.' This date is essentially a deadline in which the seller will have time to think about the offer. If they accept the offer during this time frame, then that's good – the negotiation has ended and the deal is now sealed. But when this date expires and there is still no response, it'll be perceived as seller not willing to move forward, and it will void the offer immediately. If the seller doesn't like any terms in the offer, or if there isn't enough time for the seller to consider, he/she would then have to make changes to document, along with a new acceptance date, and present back to the buyer as a counter-offer. This process will go back and forth, and the deal won't be sealed until all terms and conditions are accepted by both parties before the deadline.

Once both parties reach a mutual agreement in the deal and the negotiation is finished, the last person to make changes and/or sign the purchase and sale agreement will then need to sign a box called confirmation of execution. This confirmation will initiate the timeline for all buyers' conditions to be fulfilled, before the condition date. If they can't be fulfilled by then, both parties will either work out a time extension or the deal will be dead.

In a more complicated situation, if part of the negotiation involves fixing, you'll need to create a condition that can be fulfilled at any time. Without completing that fixing, the closing of the deal will be postponed or there might possibly be a penalty for missing the deadline. This situation definitely requires a lawyer's input so that the condition is reasonable, enforceable and legally binding.

Note that acceptance date is not the same as the condition date or completion date. Acceptance date applies to the duration of negotiation before the deal can be started. The condition date is the date by which all the sale conditions must be met (the buyer's conditions that we have previously talked about). The completion date is the time when the deal is completely closed and transfer of property procession takes place. Since completion date is the ultimate settlement date of all matters, it should be set far enough away from the condition date so that you and your lawyer will have sufficient time to do all the necessary research and paperwork.

To put things together, if you set your condition date 4 weeks from now, and your completion date 8 weeks from now, your conditional clauses will become effective today – as of the moment the confirmation of execution is signed – and will last the next 4 weeks till the condition date. During this time period, you'll get everything in place, like verification, financing, inspections, etc. Your lawyer will then have another 4 weeks (time from the condition date to the completion date) to do a title search on the property history to ensure the title is legitimate and accurate, and the property is free from any liability and litigation.

DEPOSIT FOR THE DEAL

A very important part of closing the deal is the deposit. Besides signing official documents, a purchasing transaction also requires some form of monetary exchange, so that the seller can't turn around and sell the property to another person, and you'll incur financial loss (in form of deposit) if you completely disregard any paperwork all of a sudden and walk away. Since it protects both parties, you need to put down a deposit as a sign of good faith. Many agents will try to convince (or

pressure) you to put down a significant amount, like $5000. But usually that's not necessary; in our opinion, $500 is enough. Using a large deposit can be advantageous in some circumstances. You can use it as a negotiation tactic; tell the seller you will give a much larger deposit up front if he drops his selling price slightly.

As we discussed before, the best way to negotiate is to talk with the seller directly and to understand his/her motivation to sell. If you can work out a solution that helps their needs within your capability, you're more likely to create a win-win situation and form a mutual agreement. That's why it's important to try to reach out to the seller in one way or another. And as equally important as direct communication, remember to keep your maximum price tightly to yourself and not reveal it to anyone. If the listing agent (or yours) knows what you're willing to pay for, they'll inform the seller, and they won't budge in the bargain afterwards. You'll then make the whole negotiation a lot more difficult, if not impossible, for yourself. While you only disclose from yourself information that is absolutely necessary, you always want to take the advantage of seeking others' opinions instead. For instance, you can ask your agent how much he/she feels the property will sell for. Technically, agents aren't allowed to disclose that information to you (even if they know), but they may talk openly about what they feel so you can get a ballpark of what the sale price should be.

CHAPTER 5

THINGS TO CONSIDER BEFORE REMOVING YOUR CONDITIONS

Now that your offer and deposit have been accepted, what should you do next so you can close the deal and finally take over the house?

Remember, your offer to purchase is simply an option to purchase. You can still change your mind and decide how to move the deal forward by accepting or rejecting each of the conditions one by one. In case you have any doubts or second thoughts with the deal, you can use one of those clauses as a reason to end it. But once a condition in the timeline has been accepted and waived, such as financing has been approved and you've checked the box, you can't change your mind, or go back to the offer and reject the condition in order to terminate the deal. So even though the offer provides you with options, you need to decide on each option very carefully by completing all your due diligence/homework. As we suggested before, working with a real estate attorney who is familiar with the laws and regulations of your target province can definitely help you make informed decisions.

At this stage, you have a good holistic picture of the property because you have all the accurate figures and real condition of the property. So before you check off the last condition in your offer, you should analyze the numbers (e.g. insurance, taxes, rent, etc.) again with keen eyes. If you're still satisfied with all the details, then you can waive the last condition and finalize the deal. If the numbers don't make business sense to you (e.g. not enough cash flow from rent), then you need to do something. We suggest showing your numbers/analyzer and talk frankly to the seller in a non-condescending, respectful way, so that you can start re-negotiating the deal. You're trying to make a win-win deal, but in case the seller isn't offering back what you're hoping for, it's ultimately up to you to decide how much you're willing to compromise. If you discover any problems during your homework that aren't mentioned previously in the agreement, such as actual deterioration of the furnace, this is when you need to renegotiate to have them agree to be fixed before the deal can be closed. Your lawyer will talk back and forth with the seller's lawyer to get things fixed. Once you accept and waive the last condition, your leverage on the seller will be gone, and any defects in the property will be yours to fix in the future, not the seller's.

Always be ready to walk out of the deal if the seller refuses to yield or cooperate with you in any manner. As much as you're eager to close the deal, you need to be logical (with numbers), not emotional, to make decision. At the end of the day, you're in the business for profit and long-term gain.

On the day of closing, you'll arrive at your lawyer's office with money order or cash to pay for the closing cost and the difference between financing and sale price. All legal documents will also be signed off. You will then receive the actual keys of the property – you practically own the property now! I recommend you to close the deal after the first week of the month. There are two advantages to this. Firstly, with a rental property, the seller can collect the rent for the month before you take over the property. Then, at closing, the lawyer will reduce the money you owe the seller by the rent amount, and so now you can bring less money to finish the deal. Secondly, which is more important, you don't need to rush in collecting rent on the day you close the deal. As a new property owner, you'll be in an awkward situation when you try to collect money from someone whom you don't really know. So letting the previous owner collect the rent can give you time to build relationship with the existing tenant. Try to develop a cordial relationship from day 1 by sending a really nice letter to your tenant introducing yourself and mentioning your expectations, or even meeting your tenant in person. Trust me, starting off with a positive relationship with your tenant will make your life a lot easier down the road.

After all the hard work, you're finally here, at the lawyer's office, ready to sign all documents and make the deal official. But at the table, you feel overwhelmed and terrified! Why? Because you feel you've just committed to a huge amount of money upfront, and your shoulders now have seemingly endless new responsibilities – to yourself, your investors, your lender, and your tenant. The pressure is real, but you can and you'll live up to it. As a brand new real estate investor, this nervousness is typical and understandable. But as you purchase more and more properties, you'll gain more experience, which will make things

easier. Tell yourself that if you've done all your due diligence and all numbers make business senses, and your lawyer approves of everything, then you should have confidence in your decision and feel excited with this new investment opportunity.

CHAPTER 6

MEMBERS OF YOUR SUCCESS TEAM

By now, you should have realized that, oftentimes, you need advice/help from other professionals, like realtor, inspector, and lawyer, etc. in your investment journey. As with any other businesses, you can't do everything by yourself. You need to create a team to help you succeed in the real estate business. The more professionals who can help you, the more you can delegate work that you're not good at to people who specialize in that area. Meanwhile, you can focus on finding and negotiating deals for more opportunities. For example, you can never know as much as a real estate attorney in terms of knowledge, training and experience. While you can (and should) learn about property laws and regulations so you're not out of the loop, you should definitely get help from such a legal specialist to avoid any pitfalls that you aren't even aware of. Many investors or self-employed businessmen have a "lone wolf" mentality, in which they want to do everything so they can gain full control of and profit from everything. They either think other people are less competent and don't trust them, or they're too cheap to pay for services and think they can do themselves. But in reality, the one-man-show is not a smart way to run a real estate business because you're not maximizing the use of time and talent.

If you want to get help from competent, qualified people, you need to be willing to pay them for their service. We're not saying you should choose the most expensive professional, as high price doesn't always correlate to premium quality service. But at least you should be prepared to pay fair price for the service you want. You don't want to go too low either because low price doesn't always give you the biggest bang of the buck you're hoping for. There is an old saying that "you'll get what you pay for." In this case, it's true.

THE "MUST-HAVE" PEOPLE IN YOUR TEAM

Some people are indispensable in your team formation because their strengths in specific areas of real estate industry can help you get started and grow your business. Here is a list of some of the basic people needed for your team.

Real Estate Agent / Realtor

Previously, you learned that it's possible to do everything, from hunting for property to closing the deal, without a realtor. But you've also seen that an agent is helpful in areas like paperwork preparation and during closing. So we would recommend you to use a realtor at least for your first deal, so that he/she can help you go

through the process. And if you decide to use one, make sure you get a reliable one.

How can you identify a good agent? At the minimum, he/she should be a qualified realtor who can advise you and show you the way from real-life experience, like finding and showing you relevant business numbers and analyzing whether a particular property is a good deal or not. His/her length in real estate business is actually irrelevant – your agent could be in business for 11 months or 11 years – what really makes a difference is the knowledge and negotiation skills that he/she has. Go talk to the agent, look for any proven record of success, and find out for yourself. But keep in mind, ultimately, it's still up to you to make the decision.

Preferably, you would want to work with someone who is also a real estate investor with experience in buying properties for themselves. Their experience would be most helpful to your real estate investment business because they can truly understand your needs. You may wonder why you would want to team up with people who may take all the deals for themselves. Yes, logically, you have a point, but the truth is, not all deals are good for them. As experienced investors, they may be interested in different types of properties or different scale of investment than you. That's why some deal may be fit you as a starter. Or they are interested in the same property as you, but they may lack the capital at the moment and can't get any more funding anywhere, so they would be willing to pass it on to you.

Where can you find this kind of realtor? As mentioned before, one way to find good agents is through recommendations from investors who are already successful. Once you get some names, go interview them. You can also approach some property managers, explain your needs and hopefully they'll refer you the right person. Either way, referral is your best bet and that's why networking with others in the field is so important.

When you get good realtors, you should expect them to be able to offer you an objective assessment on the house price so that you're not paying too much for it. They should also have all the necessary resources to find good properties for you, such as listings on MLS (Multiple Listing Service), and "pocket listings" (i.e. properties that aren't yet listed on MLS or won't be listed on MLS at vendors' requests).

However, you need to keep a few things in mind. First, just because the realtors don't take all those deals for themselves and pass them on to you, it doesn't necessarily mean that they're all suitable for you. For example, a property may need too much fixing that will blow you out of your budget. That's why you need to be careful and use your due diligence in screening. Second, if they're too busy on their own and only want to be responsible for finding and closing deals for you, they may not negotiate on your behalf, so it's important that you establish a direct relationship with the seller yourself. If you can't meet the seller in person, you should send a letter of introduction that explains who you are and why you're interested in purchasing the property. Third, as some realtors get paid by the seller, they're legally obliged to represent seller's interests. Only due to the contract's conditions they will also represent you. But you know the agent isn't on your side. So keep your cards close to yourself; don't disclose inner information, emotions and thoughts to any agents, even your own agent. For instance, you don't say how much you're willing to pay in the deal, and you don't want to show your love and enthusiasm for a particular property. Sellers shouldn't tell the agents their minimum sale prices, just like the buyers shouldn't tell the agents the maximum purchase prices. If they know your last cards, they'll eat you alive like sharks. During negotiation, you should always ask for everything (e.g. benefits, home appliances), even if you don't expect anything in return – of course don't tell that to your agent. Again, keep everything to yourself.

One more thing, when you go to an open house and the listing agent suggests to you a possible sale price that is much lower than the listing price, don't be surprised. It's not illegal for the agent to say that. But he/she is certainly unethical because he/she isn't representing the seller's interest properly.

Legal Team Members

While you have realtors help you with deals and numbers, you need lawyers or notary public to handle all legal matters. As a novice investor, you should let them review all the offers you make. Doing all the necessary paperwork at closing is only a part of their abilities to help you. With their legal knowledge, not only will they make sure everything on documents is legal, they will also make sure you haven't put any clauses and conditions that can put your financing and legal responsibility in jeopardy. Plus, they'll do thorough research on the history of the property so that you know the property has no outstanding liens or hidden information; in another words, the property is in good standing, so you can feel

confident in your purchase. And if you need help with financing, they can represent you and your bank/lender in creating a mortgage for the property. Of course, if a deal requires you to take out a second mortgage and it might be too risky for you, they will talk with you about that as well. That's why you need to hire a lawyer who specializes in real estate with real-life experience, not just anyone in general practice or in another field of law.

Finding a good lawyer is the same as finding a good realtor – by asking for recommendations. Legal help can be expensive, but you should resist the urge in hiring the cheapest attorney or notary in town. When you employ the wrong lawyer, you might save money at the beginning, but it will cost you a lot more than what you've saved at the end. And if you happen to find a lawyer who is also a real estate investor him/herself, that would be ideal because he/she can understand your real estate investment needs.

Property / Home Inspector

The inspector is another team member you can't live without. Even a new investor knows not to buy any property – even a brand new one – without a professional inspection because failure to inspect could have huge financial consequences down the road.

Where can you find a reliable home inspector? The search can be challenging, as different areas have their own rules and regulations. Anyone can enrol in courses from educational institutions to learn how to become a property inspector, but they may not have enough practical experience to do

the job well. Hands-on experience is very important to an inspector because the inspection itself is quite a superficial job that requires keen eyes to details and knowledge to foresee problems. In reality, the inspector isn't going to tear the walls and bathtub apart or crawl into tiny space in the basement. He/she needs to dig out hidden problems in properties – from minor issues to potential big stuff just by looking. That's when experience comes in handy.

Just like getting any other professional help, it's best to ask for referrals from other investors or realtors who have used various inspectors before. Through word of mouth and face-to-face interviews, you would be able to know who you can trust and who you should avoid. Again, resist the urge to use an inspector who charges the cheapest; you'll get what you pay for at the end.

Money Person / Mortgage Broker

Unless you're super rich where you can pay off the entire property price in full with cash, you would require lots of money to build your real estate businesses. Without it, you won't go very far. That's why the selecting of the right financing person to work with is crucial to your success. You can't do it hastily at the last minute, or simply pull a name out of the phone book, and expect that financier can help you seamlessly.

When it comes to financing, most people thought of borrowing from traditional banks right away. While you can do that, we would prefer

a mortgage broker instead because a broker can give you more financial options and flexibility (access to 50+ different lenders across the country, including private money). Especially when you can't qualify for a traditional mortgage from the banks, brokers would be your best help.

However, there are a few things about brokers you must be aware of. All mortgage brokers have access to many lenders, but that doesn't mean they can give you an advantageous rate, so you have to shop around. Some have questionable, or deceitful, business practices. Let's say if the information provided to and from the broker is wrong or illegitimate, and you fail to check that, then a year later when the lender comes back to you, you'll eventually be responsible for all the incurred costs, not the broker. Hence, your due diligence is important at all times.

One advantage a mortgage broker has over the banks is the access of private money. So ask your broker to see if he/she has access to something called the "hard-money." Hard-money is private funding that usually comes from wealthy people with lots of cash that can be lent out for loans and mortgages, or money that brokers can borrow at low interest rate, and turn around to lend you at higher interest rate so they can profit from the spread.

Essentially, hard-money lenders act like their own banks. But unlike the traditional banks, they're willing to overlook many factors or weigh them to a lesser extent, like a personal credit check. In return, you pay a premium to the lender for taking on extra risks of your loans; that is, the interest rate is considerably higher than that of the bank (e.g. 12% to 18%, plus a small percentage upfront as a finder's fee). And for riskier people or projects that are more in need of money, mortgage brokers also have access to a different source of hard-money called the subprime lenders, who will charge higher interest rate than more conventional lenders. The word 'subprime' may have a bad reputation of unethicality due to the banking industry crisis in 2008, but subprime lenders can actually be a good source of financing if you ever need them.

How do you find a good broker? Referrals, just like every other help you need! Always look for an experienced broker because only a good one is able to look at your particular deal and immediately select the top few lenders – out of a sea of lenders – that will fit your deal so you can potentially have the best available rate. From referral, also look for a broker who is an investor him/herself, so he/she can understand your business and can offer you appropriate assistance.

To be fair, even if you're working with an honest, ethical broker, you should never expect him/her to guarantee you in finding the perfect sources of financing or the lending rate you're hoping to get. Realistically, nothing can ever be ideal or happens in your way all the time. But in general, mortgage brokers are better than banks as they have more financing options and flexibility.

Other Professionals

The above types of people are the team members you absolutely need to have, at the very minimum. However, as your business grows bigger and more diverse into different types of properties, you'll realize you need more variety of professionals, such as different types of lawyers for each different types of properties,

accountant or bookkeeper for increasingly complicated financial records, and property managers and handymen to delegate your share of property fixing.

As you go into a new area of the town, or even an entirely new city, for investment opportunities, one of the first things we search for are reliable property managers and handymen. They're crucial factors in your investment strategy because you don't want to land in an area where you have no way of controlling or managing in the future. If you can't find those services, we would suggest you not to buy in that location, no matter how good the deals are.

And of course, you would want to have mentors, advisors and people you can bounce off idea with on your side at all times because their knowledge and experience are all excellent resources for your business. Plain and simple, you need trustworthy and reliable people on your team to assist you.

ADVANCED TOPICS

CHAPTER 7

HOW TO MAKE MONEY
WITH REAL ESTATE

We've created a path for you to get on this real estate boat by busting common myths and showing you the step-by-step guide in real estate investment. But to become a good real estate investor, you should expect to do hands-on work, not just knowing the theory. You need to have property management skills and people skills because you'll be actively managing your properties and tenants. Even if your business grows and you delegate some of your tasks to another property manager, you still need to keep an eye on it regularly in case you have any problems like a missing rent payment or a rowdy tenant. The problems you'll face may be discouraging and frustrating, but that's part of running your own business.

Now thinking deeper, you may wonder why real estate is an important, if not number one, long-term investment choice for you in the first place. As you may have already seen in this book, real estate can offer you financial security and lucrative profitability, even in an economic slump. In fact, it's one of the safest investment instruments when it's purchased and managed properly.

Don't believe me? Just look at some of the world's richest people – Ka-Shing Li and Donald Trump are prime examples – they started to make money and continue to hold their wealth throughout their lives! Real estate is a relatively low risk way to generate cash flows, which creates a reliable safety net for you and your family. It would especially become beneficial after your retirement, when you need a steady passive income the most, in order to supplement your pension. But keep in mind that we're talking about "long-term" investment, not house-flipping after holding it for a year or two. Real estate investment should not be viewed as a get-rich-quick scheme, but a get-rich slow process. To get the maximum benefit, you need to treat it like a business with a long term horizon in mind.

Specifically, there are at least 7 reasons why real estate investment can earn you profits. In real estate investment terms, we call those reasons profit centers.

PROFIT CENTER # 1: IMMEDIATE EQUITY

Unless you're in a very hot market with less/no room for negotiation, you can make money as soon as you buy a property, and we're not even joking you. Let's say you purchase a property at 10% below listed market value. That means you've created 10% immediate equity. In number terms, if a house is listed for $300,000 on the market, and today you successfully buy it for $270,000. You've just created $30,000 of immediate equity on your net worth statement.

Of course you may have doubt about this and ask, "Why would anyone ever want to sell his/her property at a discount with 40% or more?" Oftentimes, homeowners are willing to sell their houses at a price below market value because of urgency or unfavourable situations, such as divorce, job loss or transfer, inability to make mortgage payments and fear of foreclosure, and deteriorating property condition. You should note that a run-down property is still worth a purchase if you can get it at a very deep discount. The idea is to buy one at a price that is way, way below market value, which allows you to put in some serious renovation to turn it around, and then still sell it below fair market value to earn some immediate equity.

If you have the ability to close a deal quickly, you can generally get a substantial discount on the purchase price. Remember, most people that NEED to sell have to sell fast!

We recently bought a small condominium in a residential high rise building. The unit was on the main floor with its own separate entrance, and was located at 12837- 66 street NW in Edmonton, Alberta. We actually found it in an online ad, which was advertised for $60,000. It was a recent foreclosure that was taken back by the previous owner because the owner did not keep up with his mortgage payments. It was also in desperate need of cleaning as a denturist was using it as his office. Plus, there was a $2000 special assessment from the condominium corporation that was due. At the end, we made an all cash offer of $55,000 with a two week closing time, and the seller was responsible for paying the special assessment. That meant we purchased the property for about 10% under listed price. Not bad for a small deal like this. However, it is actually, significantly better. The cities tax records indicated that the property was currently assessed at over $80,000 and the market value is closer to $100,000. That means we actually purchased the property at about 30 to 45% discount from the true value.

PROFIT CENTER # 2: PROPERTY APPRECIATION

This is the most common way a property can profit you. In the short term, housing prices do have fluctuations, so it's normal to see a rise and fall in pricing. But in the long run, house values will appreciate. For example, five years ago, you bought a house for $300,000, and today you successfully sell it for $350,000. That means, over the course of 5 years, your house value has appreciated by $50,000, and that's the profit you've made from the house just by owning it. Most home owners are actually real estate investors, they just do not know it! For most people, they buy a house and then just live in it for the next 20 or 30 years, and all that time it is just sitting there appreciating. It is not uncommon for someone to have bought their home for $50,000 20 years ago, and now have that property worth over $500,000. That is a 10 times increase in value over 20 years, or a 13% per year compounded rate of return for doing nothing but living in the property!

However, as good as it sounds, in order to get profit from appreciation, it requires you to purchase the property at the right time. Hence, if you buy a property only with the hope for appreciation to earn your profit and disregard timing in purchase, your strategy is called speculating, not investing. That's not what this book is advocating. This is why many people were caught when the bubble burst in 2007. They were gambling on pure appreciation over a short time and were devastated when the prices actually dropped, and they could no longer afford to hold on to the property, because they had purchased it while it had a negative cash flow.

PROFIT CENTER # 3: STEADY CASH FLOW

Having cash flow is paramount in the investment world because you can reinvest to generate even more cash flow. In real estate, this means you should never buy any property that can't generate positive cash flow (i.e. profit after all the expenses). For example, if you charge $1500 for monthly rent, and at the end of each month, after you deduct all the expenses, including tax and mortgage, you're left with $100 of monthly profit, that'll be the positive cash flow that we're talking about.

As difficult as the housing market is – like in large metropolitan cities – you should never invest in properties that are cash flow negative. Even if the house isn't generating any positive cash flow, you need to charge enough rent to break even at the very least; your tenant will pay off your mortgage and all the expenses, and you can rely on the property's natural appreciation. Regardless of where you live, you can always get investment properties that are cash flow positive. But if you really can't find one in prime locations or your desired neighbourhood, then look into suburbs or find an area that will work for you. The bottom line is: positive cash flow is king.

Back in 2007, people who purchased property properly and had positive cash flow were NOT really hurt when the bubble burst, because they could just keep holding on to their properties till the market recovered. However, people who had negative cash flowing properties (meaning they had to pay every month) could not afford to hold to their properties for very long. That is why there were so many foreclosures at that time.

PROFIT CENTER # 4: MORTGAGE PRINCIPAL REDUCTION

Once you have a mortgage from the bank, you'll need to make monthly mortgage payments. At the beginning of the mortgage, a significant amount of your payment will pay for the interest, and remaining small percentage of 2% to 4% will go to reduce the principal amount. This principal reduction is called silent cash because you do not really see it or even notice it. That debt reduction amount becomes your profit even though you don't physically see it, and you need to include it in your taxable income.

So, in the example of a $300,000 property with 10% down payment, you'll have a mortgage of $270,000. The mortgage is reduced in the first year by, say, 5%, which is $13,500. A $13,500 decrease in debt is now a $13,500 increase in equity, and that's your profit.

PROFIT CENTER # 5: FINANCIAL LEVERAGE

As a new investor without a lot of cash, you often use a loan from a lender to buy a property. Imagine you can control 100% of a property with just 10% down payment, this leverage is an enormous advantage of real estate investment; you get to control a huge asset with very little of your own cash.

Let's say you put $20,000 in stock market and get 5% return on investment, you earn $1,000. But if you invest the same $20,000 in a $300,000 property that will appreciate 5%, you'll profit 5% of $300,000, which is $15,000. With $20,000 down payment, you earn $15,000, that's 75% return on investment. Now $1,000 versus $15,000, what would you choose? Now let's say rather than using your own $20,000 to invest, you get an investor to come in with the cash, and you end up paying them $5,000 for the money. The investor is making 25% return ($5,000/$20,000) on their money (which is great for them)! However, your return is now much better, in fact it is infinitely better! That is because you now have NONE of your own money into the project and have made the remaining $10,000 profit. $10,000 return with $0 invested gives you an infinite return! This is why financial investors are a key to your financial success.

PROFIT CENTER # 6: ALLOWABLE DEPRECIATION

We just said appreciation is a good thing for you as an investor, so if I say depreciation is also a positive thing, it would seem counter-intuitive to you. But indeed it is!

Most governments allow homeowners to depreciate their properties even though their values appreciate in reality. As houses get older, say 25-plus years, many problems will start to surface, like leaky roof, faulty furnace, and weaken house structure. So with natural deterioration in mind, the government allows yearly property depreciation at 4%, so that you can reduce your annual taxable income by that depreciating part of the property value. Let's say your house has a market value of $350,000, in which the land is worth $50,000 and the physical building is worth $300,000, which is the replacement value of the building. The government will then allow you to take the replacement value of $300,000 and reduce it annually by 4% (i.e. $12,000 in this year) until the value goes down to zero. Now, during tax season, you can apply that $12,000 to lower your taxable income that the property generates for the year, and then use those tax savings for other purposes, like reinvesting into another property. Some people call this saving the "phantom money" or "deferred saving" because eventually you have to pay the accumulated amount back to the government when you sell the property. But the nice thing about using depreciation on your taxes as an expense is that it usually offsets the profits from mortgage payments!

As you just saw, you can use depreciation to your advantage. But I strongly recommended you to seek an accountant's advice and see if it's worthwhile for you to do so for tax purposes.

PROFIT CENTER # 7: REINVESTMENT POSSIBILITY

Other than renting out your property to earn steady cash flows, you can also refinance it and reinvest the money. Let's say you're living in a house that is worth $350,000 and it's all paid off with no debt. While it's great that the house is all paid off, it's also not doing anything for you as a homeowner; your house has become dead equity.

You decide to take out a line of credit against your house for $50,000 at 3%. You then lend the money to an investor at 11%. So the investor is paying you $5,500 in interest every year, and you're paying the bank $1,500 for annual interest. Essentially, you're making $4,000 of profit in a year without doing anything other than leveraging your home. Is that amazing? Now what is your rate of return? Is it $4,000/$50,000 = 26.7%, right?

Many of the investors we deal with use this exact method of reinvestment to make money. They take equity out of their existing properties and use that money to invest with us into other cash-flowing properties that give a safe, consistent return on their money. If you would like to receive more information on this kind of deals, please contact us directly to discuss about any investment opportunities we currently have available for you.

CHAPTER 8

HOW TO MANAGE YOUR PROPERTY

Once you've got your investment property, managing a physical house itself isn't that difficult; when something breaks down or doesn't work, you go fix it or hire someone else to do it. But as your portfolio increases in size, keeping all your relationships healthy with tenants, handymen and contractors and being able to communicate and cooperate is a lot harder. So it's fair to say that, in property management, managing people is as equally important as managing properties; the two components are in one inseparable package. Property management is where people skills are required the most.

HOME MANAGEMENT

As a homeowner, when we talk about home management, we refer to managing the actual house and all of its related operations, like bill payments, fixing, etc. Before you outsource home management duties to a third party, you should try to manage the house yourself for at least 6 to 12 months, so that you know what is involved in taking care of a house, and what to expect from a property manager. Even after you've hired someone as your property manager, you still need to maintain vigilance and control of the operation, such as proper budget and expenditure, and punctual bill payments.

Before your new tenant moves in, you need to manage your house proactively by going to the unit and repairing all defects you can find. This will ensure your house is in excellent condition to begin with. In contrast, if there are problems, like leaking taps or insufficient insulation, and you choose to ignore them, not only will they cost you a lot more in water or heating bills, they will also send the new tenants a wrong message that you as a homeowner don't even care. You think your tenants will in turn take care of the house for you? Most likely not. But if you keep your house in good shape, you can attract decent, responsible tenants who can save you money in the long run with fewer damages from them. If you're lucky, they might be nice enough to do some repairs and maintenance work for you at their expenses!

Once your house is all ready for the tenants, walk through the entire house with them and do a thorough inspection to make sure they're happy with the condition. Make sure you document everything and have both parties' signatures on the report; that will become a proof of the initial condition of the property. With any damages afterwards, you know they're caused by the tenants, and you'll have legal ground to demand for compensations or fixing, depending on the severity of the damage. If it's something small like cigarette burns in carpet or holes in the wall, you can either let your tenants fix it themselves, or ask them to pay for the cost of your repairs. For something bigger, definitely go after them for compensation. But without documentation, it'll be difficult to prove that the damages are in fact from the tenants.

Other than the initial inspection, you also need to set up a regular schedule for property inspection in the contract. Inspection should be carried out at least once a year, or better yet, 2 to 4 times a year. A very good excuse for an inspection is to drop by and pick up the rent checks. When you do that you will get a sneak peek into the condition of your property without actually doing a full inspection. You may question if the frequency is too much. From our experience, four times a year is actually reasonable; not only can you detect problems before they get worse and extend the life of your house; you can also daunt any potential illegal activities from taking place, like growing marijuana in the basement. When you discover any defects or deterioration, such as leaky taps and toilets, and faulty windows and doors, try to repair them within a week. You can really impress your tenants with your efficiency and care.

One particular area to pay attention is your smoke detectors. You should inspect them (testing and changing battery if needed) at least twice a year. To make it easier to remember, you can do it before every seasonal change in fall and spring. Why are smoke detectors so important? It's because, without any inspection and have tenant signed off the report, there's no proof that you have functional smoke detectors in your property. In case of a fire accident, carbon monoxide leaks, or even a loss of life, you'll be held legally liable with negligence as landlord, facing penalty of fines and/or jail time. The best thing to do is to have one smoke detector on every floor, including the basement. Your local fire department is a good source of information if you have any questions or concerns.

PEOPLE MANAGEMENT

Managing a home is easy; you can set up schedules and protocols to fulfill any necessary, or even tedious, duties – all you have to do is to act on them diligently. Managing people, however, is a lot more difficult because humans are more dynamic with different backgrounds, personalities, preferences, and mentality. You need to deal with a lot more interpersonal variables simultaneously and communicate in a way that can gain mutual understanding and cooperation.

The rule of thumb in tenant management is to establish a good relationship with them. However, under this notion, there's a difference between running a business and a social club, and that's the fine line you shouldn't cross. You should always to be courteous and respectful to your tenants, but you cannot make friends with them. Once you befriend them, they will then have a tendency of not living up to your expectation on them. For example, if they're late in rent payment, or fail to maintain your house properly, they will expect you to overlook that and forgive them. It'll become a vicious cycle: they don't behave properly, you'll need to forgive them, they know they can get away with it and won't comply even more. Essentially, at that stage, you lose all your power to govern as a landlord and won't be able to manage your business like a business. The bottom line is, mixing business with friendship is a big no-no! Be FAIR but FIRM and treat tenants in a business-like fashion!

The first step in building a good relationship for your business more easily is to work with right candidates that fit you. Hence, you need to learn how to screen and qualify tenants and fish out the ones that can work with you. As a new landlord without much experience, you should seek out your network, like real estate investor club or landlord association, for advice and resources. It's much safer and more time-efficient for you to learn from other people's mistakes than to learn by making those mistakes yourself. For instance, when you create a screening questionnaire to ask your potential tenant on the phone or in-person, there are things that you can and cannot ask. Your connections can give you help and tips on that. Based on the answers to the questions, you can feel if a particular candidate is someone you want to rent your house to. Do their occupations give them enough financial stability for the rent? How self-responsible are they for their lives? What kind of lifestyle do they have? Those are some example insights you may want to know about a prospect in your preliminary assessment. Once you decided on some clients, send them an application form asking for their personal information and permission to do a credit check on them.

Speaking of application form, it may be better if you have your real estate attorney created it because different jurisdictions have different rules and regulations on information privacy act. And remember, if you do seek legal help, you need to hire an attorney who specializes in tenant-landlord relationship, not just any lawyers. If not, you can google one online, or reach out to landlord association or real estate investor club for more information.

With credit checks, there are two ways of doing it. One way is to do the credit check by yourself. You can subscribe to an online credit check service, such as RentCheck Credit Bureau. Once you register yourself as a landlord and pay an annual fee, you can then submit client's information to the website and they'll send you a credit check report on the client. There are a few of those service sites out there, so before you use one, we would recommend you to first browse around and read customers' reviews/comments on them, or check with Better Business Bureau (BBB). Another way is to let a third party do the credit check for you. This method, however, requires you to get permission from your prospect beforehand, stating that their application forms will be shared with third parties, and it's solely for the purpose of checking their debt payments history. Once you get their okay, you can then send your client's application form to your mortgage broker for a credit check.

Previously, we talked about the fact that you can't always rely on home sellers' information; it's best to assume that their numbers aren't always correct, and hence, you should do your due diligence. The same holds true for potential tenants; it's best to assume the information they give you on the application forms is incorrect. That's why, during your assessment of their application forms, or your interview with them, you need to be thorough and vigilant in order to find out their real backgrounds. One good way to check is to follow up on the references they provide you. But of course, you're not going to ask the reference how the prospects are because, chances are, their answers are always in favour of the prospects. After all, why would a prospect provide you with a reference that would speak badly about him/her? So you can use a trick to test the credibility of the reference. The point is to give out some false information to test the reference. If his friend is posing as Mr. Smith's reference, he would agree

with whatever information you say, and you know the reference is lying. But if the reference corrects you by telling you the correct information then you know the reference is legitimate.

In your application, you should ALWAYS ask for more than one previous rental reference. You should ask for their current landlords contact information as well as at least one more previous landlord. And then, you should contact all of them! Contacting the current landlord is pretty much a waste of time; you generally cannot trust anything they say as they have a vested interest. If the person is a good tenant and they want to keep them, they will tell you that they are a horrible person who never pays their rent on time, since they do not want the tenant to find a new place. If they are a horrible tenant the current landlord will probably tell you they are the absolute best tenants who actually pay their rent early. That is because they want you to rent to them so they can get rid of them. The previous landlord has no vested interest in the situation and will probably give you the truth.

Other than checking references, you can also judge people by how they appear (e.g. clothing, watch) and speak (e.g. mannerism), and whom they hang out with (e.g. social life). While it might sound superficial (and horrible) that I'm telling you to judge a book by its cover, oftentimes, without knowing a person for a significant amount of time, any clues that a person displays can give you a gut feeling of who he/she is. For example, if your potential tenant comes to see your apartment in his dirty rustbucket with food crumbs, beer cans and trash all over his car, would you have faith in him taking care of your property? Probably not – you think he'll treat it the same way as his car.

There is one more consideration in tenant-landlord relationship when it comes to leases. Since different areas have different requirements in creating a lease, you must provide tenants things that your area's lease requires you to provide. Although you can't make additional changes that'll change the nature of it, you can add your own rules and regulations to the lease contract. For instance, if your tenants want to keep a pet in your property, it's up to you to decide whether you allow them to do so or not. If you do, you can set your own extra fee and rules, and list them out in an addendum, and attach it to the initial lease. Before you finalize it, you should let your attorney take a look at it to ensure the legality of your addendum in your province and in case there's a dispute with your tenants.

GOOD TENANTS VS. BAD TENANTS

As hard as you try to screen your prospects, you'll always encounter some horrible tenants who are not the people they initially appear to be. Based on our experience, generally, out of 100 tenants, you'll get 5% who are excellent without any problems whatsoever, 15% who are terrible and will make your life like a living hell, and the rest 80% is your average type of tenants who may have some issues occasionally, but overall they aren't too difficult to work with.

If you happen to get good tenants, you must treat them nicely to reward them because those tenants aren't easy to come by. The paramount way is to keep your house in good shape by checking and making prompt repairs. Not only can you extend the life of your house, you've also created a home where your tenants will feel comfortable living in; their kindness is rewarded with a happy home. As we have previously mentioned you don't want to get too close to them personally, but you should always be polite, respectful, and responsive. And to really good tenants, you can even make them happy with small gestures like birthday card, Christmas card, and anniversary card of the lease. The bottom line is, it's cheaper with less hassle to keep the current good tenants than to find a new one who might not be as good. The best thing we ever did was at Christmas time. We went to a local grocer and got small turkeys at a bulk price, and then gave every tenant a turkey for their Christmas dinner. For a few hundred dollars, we had the best tenants believable for the next year.

On the flip side, good landlords are as hard to come by as good tenants. If your tenants like dealing with you, they may stay with you even if your rent is $30-$50/month higher than the market rate. So don't underestimate the power of a good relationship.

Also, treating tenants well can have a beneficial effect in the long run. One day, when your tenants move out, they may leave your house in a much better connection than before, which would be great. And if they say nice things about you to their connections and in the community, that will help build up your positive reputation as a landlord. Through word of mouth and recommendation, it may be easier for you to find new quality tenants.

When you have multiple tenants in different units, beware not to fall into the trap of playing favourites. People talk to each other all the time. If they find out you're more responsive to one tenant's problems than the others, they'll compare and hold grudge on you. So it's very important that you need to be nice and fair to everyone. Just think about how you would react if you were discriminated against.

In the case where you're unlucky and still have bad tenants after your due diligence, you have to know how to make them play by your rules. The most common problem is late rent payment. It's important to learn that late rent payment absolutely cannot be tolerated, not even for a few days, and not even if she's an old lady who gives you free fruits every time she sees you. You may think I sound so harsh and insensitive to others, but there is a reason for acting promptly. On the day your tenant is supposed to pay rent but fails to do so, you need to present him an official notice of tenancy termination, stating that if he misses his rent today, he has 14 days to pay it. After that, you'll apply to the court for his eviction. If he pays within 14 days, the document will get filed away and everything goes back to normal. But if you don't act immediately right on the first day, not only will you delay the rent collection, you'll also delay your time of pursuing legal actions against him.

To pre-empt this situation, we generally have late payment clauses in all our leases, so that when a payment is late or their payment does not clear, the tenant is also responsible for an additional fee for each case. Make specific that if a payment does NOT clear, it will then also be considered late and both fees will be applicable.

Another great idea is using the concept of reduced rent. You make the lease for a rental amount that is higher than the rent you want, BUT as long as the rent is paid on time there is a discount applied. So if they ever miss a rental payment, the rent automatically adjusts to the higher amount from that point on. It is a great incentive to pay on time.

With a sweet old lady, you should go gently on her while remaining assertive. You should deliver the notice to her in person – not by mail, slide it under the door, or put it in the mailbox – and explain that this is a standard procedure. By doing this in person, you're covering your ground in case she really doesn't pay the rent and you have to evict her eventually. A common excuse tenants give in court to get an extension is that they never received the notice. If you give it to them in person, they cannot use that as an excuse. Being assertive, yet polite, is important so that she'll learn your bottom line and she knows she can't manipulate you with being an old granny. At the end of the day, you're running a business, not a charity.

Regardless of the nature and severity of a problem, whether it's about rent or noise complaints from neighbour, you need to document absolutely everything whenever a problem arises. You need to collect all those information in order to build a legitimate profile of evidence, so you can use it in case you do have to face your tenant in court one day. From our experience, troubled tenants tend to be chronic troublemakers because they fail to realize they've been causing problems and hence do not change their behaviours. Oftentimes, legal action might be the only solution, and that's why thorough documentation is very important.

Physical proof like photos and videos is the best kind of evidence to be used in court. But keep in mind that, as much as you want during your inspection, you legally can't go into your property and take photos or videos without your tenant's permission. If they refuse to allow you, you can't do it. The best way to do this is to start with it during the initial property inspection on move in. Good tenants should never have a problem with you recording the initial property inspection on video. If they do have a problem with it, you may be in for troubles in the future!

The worst type of problem you can encounter from tenant is the illegal marijuana growing operations, often known as "grow-op." They're huge problems for landlords because they can ruin or completely destroy your property – from stains and smell around the house to the underlying structure of the property. Yet, there is no insurance to protect the homeowner against the damages incurred in case your tenant carries out that kind of operation in your house. Since you bear the full financial liability without any help, in order to protect yourself, you need to include a clause in your rental contract that gives you the right to inspect your house on a monthly basis. You most likely won't need to check on your tenants that frequently, but this clause will deter any criminals from renting your unit in the first place, as they want to avoid people scrutinizing them. The bottom line is, whenever you feel suspicious, check your property monthly and immediately.

Another clause I like putting in my rental agreements is a termination clause due to illegal activity, which allows you to terminate the tenancy if there is ever any illegal activity on the property.

CHAPTER 9

HOW TO PURCHASE PROPERTY WITH NONE OF YOUR OWN MONEY

You'll definitely doubt me when you see the title of this chapter. You might ask, "Is it really possible to purchase properties without investing any of your own money, or are you just boasting?" The truth is, yes, it is possible, but you need to get funding from somewhere; it could come from a bank or a private lender.

Everyone has heard the phrase "no money down deal"; that does not mean there is no money put down on the deal. It simply means that the money does NOT come from you. You incorporate other sources of capital rather than your own wallet.

After the experience of your first property as an investor and landlord, you feel you're ready to expand your business by buying more properties. Now the problem is that you have no more money for any down payments after your first property. What can you do? The most straight-forward way of thinking is that you should wait to save up for down payment for your next investment. You can save up for your next property by using funds from, employment or cash flows from your first property. But in reality, as a smart investor, you don't have to and you don't want to go that way because you'll be missing great opportunities in the meantime.

Let's say your first property is worth $300,000 in which $60,000 (20% of house value) was your down payment. A year later, you see this amazing deal that you don't want to miss out but you don't have another $60,000 down payment for this second property.

You now have a couple of different options to get the down payment. One option to get the required capital is to do an equity take-out from your first property by taking out a second mortgage on it. Remember your down payment of $60,000 for your first property? That's the equity that you can take out for your next purchase. Here is what you do to set up a second mortgage: you approach another investor who is looking for 7% to 10% return on his/her investment and is willing to lend you the $60,000. You'll borrow that amount against the first property as a mortgage, and apply it to your second purchase. Your first and best choice here is to find an investor yourself who is interested in dealing with you to get a safe secure return on their money, and have that investment secured by a mortgage on a piece of real estate. We routinely offer these types of mortgages to our investors. If you currently have some capital to invest, then please contact us directly to find out about current opportunities we may have available. Alternatively, you can contact your mortgage broker as they routinely deal in second mortgages from bans and private investors.

This arrangement is amazing because you now own 100% of the second property without your own money. You can definitely use your first property as a leverage to get a second mortgage for your next property.

The second option is to find a partner who can lend you $60,000 to buy the property, and eventually split the profit in half. Splitting your profit 50/50 with a partner is quite common, so after you do 2 deals, you'll essentially get one property for free. Even if you only get to keep 20% of profits within the partnership, when you do 5 deals with 20% return of investment (ROI) each, you'll be getting 100% of profit on your fifth deal. However, it's common for new investors to have the old 'lone wolf' mentality where they want to handle everything all by themselves. It's definitely doable, but you're making your life harder and your business growth a lot slower. One way to quickly create wealth is to maximize the leverage of other people's expertise, experience and money. It's true that all wealthy investors started out slowly and modestly, sometimes on their own to begin with. But eventually they learned how to grow and expand their businesses with partnerships to grow their resources. You can be sure that no successful investor would ever only rely on his/her own capital for their businesses.

It looks like you can gain a lot from partnership, which makes people wonder why they would ever want to partner up with you and lend you the down payment in the first place. What's the benefit for them? There may be several reasons. For instance, your partner may be interested in real estate investment but has no such knowledge in the field, or he/she may be a busy professional who has no time to go through the whole process in property purchase. Either way, your partner would benefit from your knowledge and experience in real estate, so there are mutual benefits for both of you.

Where can you find a partner? Your family and friends would be a good start. But personally, I generally do not like dealing with family as investors, they tend to be too demanding and they will always second guess your decisions.

Keep your eyes and ears open and talk to the people you know or meet on a regular basis, or professionals who service you use like doctors, nurses, mechanics, etc. Regardless of who you talk to, you'll always appear more trustworthy and convincing when you become an expert in real estate yourself; the more knowledge, experience, and dedication you have in the field, the more likely you can attract investors to join your boat.

Although you may prefer to work with a single investor to make things easy, you can always have more than one partner. The benefit of multiple partnerships is that if you need to raise a large amount, say $100,000, for down payment, it will definitely be more manageable for people to get involve when you split it up among five people rather than just two.

One point you can always mention to your potential partners is that, in Canada, they can invest in real estate through their personal RRSP (Registered Retirement Savings Plan) self-directed fund account. They can take those funds in the account out of the general markets and self-direct them into real estate. It's worth bringing this to their attention because most people don't know that. Our next chapter it dedicated to this subject.

Another point you should explain to your investors is how ROI is calculated and what ROI is expected from partnership. Quantifying information with numbers is always a better way than just words to impress people. That's why it is very important for you to understand various investment concepts, terminology, and calculations so that you can demonstrate to your potential investors what they can gain when they partner up with you. The more you can educate them, the more willing they are going to join you in your real estate business.

Based on personal experience, not all of those people you approach will turn out to be your partners, so don't be disappointed if they reject your invite for partnership. Instead, you should feel good about helping people with your teaching, and hope that one day they'll change their minds and invest with you, or offer you help when you are in need, or refer you to other people in their networks. That's why networking is so important. Networking may seem intimidating, especially with strangers, but it's actually not difficult to connect people via teaching. You don't hand out business card to everyone in the room either. When you go to any kind of events, your goal is to meet and make a good, meaningful connection with just one person instead of meeting superficially with 10 people. Through that one person, you'll start to know all the people in his/her network, which will create a large network of money.

At the end, regardless of how many fellow investors you're working with, it's extremely important to maintain good relationships with them. One way to treat them well is to give them an above average ROI, so they're happy to stay in partnership with you. When it comes to time to sell your investments, make sure you give them their fair shares of profits. If you build a reputation of being a good business partner, soon the words will get out, and opportunities will flood into your door.

CHAPTER 10

USING YOUR RRSP TO INVEST IN REAL ESTATE

A lot of people invest in paper assets (e.g. mutual funds, stocks, and bonds) with their personal RRSP accounts, but they seldom know that real estate is also an investment vehicle available for their RRSP money. Although the process of using RRSP for real estate is more complicated, it's worth exploring this option to open more doors for your investments.

In order to invest in real estate using your RRSP account, you first need to put your RRSP money in a self-directed fund that allows you to decide where you can invest with your money. To do that, you need to sell off and move your RRSP fund from your current financial product to a money market fund within your financial institution. The money market fund is like a cash account, but within the RRSP portfolio. From the money market fund, you'll then move

your RRSP funds to a trust company that will allow you to redirect your funds to your own preferred investment vehicle, whatever that may be.

Once your money is in self-directed account, you can then become a private lender, which lets you lend to investors looking for cash. For example, if an investor approaches you with an offer of a second mortgage to invest in his property and you're interested in it, you and the investor will negotiate the ROI and final payment for you at the end of the agreement term, and you'll then put your RRSP fund into the second mortgage. This would now become a great investment for you as a lender because your money will be earning a rate that you're happy with and is secured against a real physical property.

If you happen to be on the investor side looking for cash, this would become a great option to raise capital, as you can do it without going through the bank for conventional refinancing. You put a second mortgage on your house, and someone put his RRSP on it – a match with mutual benefit. However, whether you should partner up with another person for a second mortgage, or refinance your house with a new larger first mortgage to replace the original mortgage, you'll have to evaluate the pros and cons of each option.

CHAPTER 11

PRIVATE MORTGAGE

We have previously talked about private mortgages and how they are a great way to raise money to purchase real estate with. But many people do not know that private mortgages are also good investments. If you are somebody that has idle cash sitting in the bank doing absolutely nothing and getting your 0.5% a year return from saving accounts or GICs, you might want to consider investing your money into private mortgages. A private mortgage is an investment that is secured by a mortgage on the title of the property you are investing in. It allows you to get a decent, safe, and consistent return over an extended period of time. Investing your money into private mortgages essentially allows you to play the function of a bank. Since we all know the banks make lots of money with the investments they do, so why not become the bank yourself?

The terms of typical private mortgages range between 1 to 5 years and, in some cases, even longer. Interest rates on private mortgages span a full spectrum anywhere from 4% to 12% per year and sometimes even higher. The major determining factors are the length of term for the mortgage and whether or not the mortgage is a first mortgage, second mortgage, or even third mortgage. The typical interest rate for first mortgages is around 3% to 5%, for second mortgages anywhere between 4% and 8%, and for third mortgages anywhere from 6% to 12%. These are some of the typical rates that we offer our investors who choose to invest private money with us on various real estate projects. If you have readily available cash and are interested in getting safe secure consistent returns like this, please contact us and we can let you know the available opportunities that we currently have.

Many people do not realize that there is also another way to invest with mortgages and make a greater return than just the interest rate on the mortgage itself. This method or technique involves purchasing mortgages at a discount. Most people do not know that mortgages can be bought and sold just like any other assets. Once a mortgage is placed on a property, it then becomes an asset that can be manipulated. Similar to a piece of property that is bought and sold on the open market, mortgages can be dealt with the same way. As such, you can find occurrences where you can purchase a mortgage at a discount. You may not think this is possible, but remember our previous discussion about discounted properties, and you will quickly realize that you can actually achieve significant discounts when purchasing a mortgage. Many real estate transactions involve the seller holding a second mortgage on the property that they have sold, which makes it easier for them to sell the property. However, they do not realize some of their return for a few years after the property is sold when the mortgage term expires and the mortgage is paid out. If that person is desperate for cash for whatever reason, they might consider selling that mortgage at a discount in order to generate a quick sale. A mortgage with a listed interest rate of 6% can give you anywhere from 6% return, if you purchase it at face value, up to 12% or even higher return, depending on how much of a discount you initially purchased the mortgage for.

Here, we will show you an example that we did on a property located at 6501 - 47th Street in Wetaskiwin, Alberta. This second mortgage was due October, 2016 and had a value of $135,000 with an interest rate of 6% but gave us a return of 24% when we purchased it.

The mortgage was established by the previous vendor of the property who took back a vendor take-back mortgage on the property for a number of years in order to expedite the sale of the property. In December of 2015, we contacted the holder of the mortgage whom we knew was in desperate need of some readily available cash. The mortgage was for $135,000 at 6%, which meant that it had monthly payments of $675 per month. In December of 2015, we offered the mortgage holder the amount of $100,000 to purchase his mortgage. After some negotiation, we settled on a purchase amount of $120,000 for his $135,000 mortgage. Then, all we had to do was wait till the mortgage comes due in October of 2016, and we would make $15,000 on my $120,000 investment. That results in a return of 12.5%. But in reality, our returns are actually more. While we're waiting for the mortgage to mature in October, we're receiving monthly payments of $675 a month for the next 10 months. That results in an additional total of $6,750, and over the next 10 months, we're receiving a total of $21,750 ($15,000 from the mortgage purchase and $6,750 from the monthly payments). So now, our total return of $21,750 on an investment of $120,000 results in an effective interest rate of 18%. However, that is not for an entire year. That is only over a 9 month period from January 2016 to October 2016. If you annualize that return out over an entire year, that results in an annual interest rate of approximately 24% per year. Not bad from a mortgage that only shows a 6% return!

CHAPTER 12

RENOVATING YOUR PROPERTY

After you've closed a deal, you officially own the underlying property. If you're a do-it-yourself type of handyman who has been fixing things around the house, then good for you, you most likely know some basics about renovation. But if you've never done a renovation before because you hired other people or companies to do it, then it's time for you to learn if you want to succeed in the real estate business.

Renovation is an aspect of investment that requires the most time, dedication and effort to learn. However, once you learn it well, it'll become your biggest source of revenue. When you wholesale a property, less work will be on your shoulders, as renovation will be taken care of by the other investor. But this in turn means the other investor would need to have a high enough margin to make a profit, and hence, your profit margin will have to be cut lower. That's why it's a good idea to learn how to renovate properties so you can

keep more profits in your wallet from each deal, and know how to manage renovation crews and their progress.

Your knowledge and experience in renovation can give you flexibility in handling various kinds of deals. Let's say you encounter a property that is selling at a very deep discount, but it has many problems associated with it (e.g. a run-down home) and the owner wants to get rid of it in a matter of few days. You can try to wholesale it. But this strategy might not work in such a short period of time, unless you already have a long list of buyers. With your knowledge and experience in renovation, you can buy and make over the property. Otherwise, you'll have no choice but to miss out on this opportunity.

Knowing property renovation can also give you confidence in negotiating with investors who are also experienced renovators. When you can give your investor accurate information about the amount of work required and the true value after renovation, he/she will trust your assessment and competency, so that you'll be able to negotiate for a higher price in a deal with your credibility. You see how renovation knowledge can give you a competitive advantage over other investors?

And when you do a good job fixing up a property, not only do you add values to the house, your work will benefit the local community as well. Without a doubt, the price of your newly remodelled home will significantly be higher than an ugly, run-down property, but the presence of your new house will also improve the values of other houses and the overall image of the neighbourhood. The community will thank you for your work!

However, as a starter, I wouldn't recommend that you take on properties that require major renovation from top to bottom, unless you have previous interior design and construction experience. You should start learning by renovating a property with very small and simple problems. Not only are those properties manageable for your experience level, they're also some of the easiest deals to finish. As you gain more hand-on experience in renovation, you can tackle more complicated properties.

THE RENOVATION PROCESS

It's important to have a system for renovation in place because it allows you to remotely handle multiple renovation projects simultaneously and free up your time more for deal hunting. Although renovation is a very extensive area to learn, we'll break down the process in various steps, so that you can at least gain a general overview of the process.

Step 1: Developing A Scope of Work

First, you'll need to create a scope of work because it's the key to the success of your project. This checklist will guide you (and your contractors) through all the items that you need to renovate for the property, listed by different sections of the house. Under each item, you'll also list the materials you want to use, along with their SKU numbers and estimated costs. When your contractors look at the checklist, they should be able to visualize what the finished property will look like, anticipate what work is needed, and hence, figure out how to bid for your job. Since everything is standardized and laid out clearly, it'll be easier for you to compare with different bids from contractors and look for better pricing. The list is also used as a step-by-step reference to monitor the renovation progress and formulate the payment schedule for your contractors, so that you can avoid miscommunication and disputes during renovation, and save you money and time down the road. Once you have the scope or work ready, you should take it with you, along with the following items when you visit the property:

Advertising materials – Take advantage of free promotional opportunities for your business by putting up signs and banner on the property's windows or roof, or on the front lawn. Let the neighbourhood know you're in the business to buy and renovate houses.

Camera – You need to take photos for the "before" condition of the property for two reasons. First, your potential property buyers will want to see the renovations that you claim you've done. Those photos will become the best proof of your work when the buyers can see and compare the "before" and "after" conditions. Second, if you list your remodelled home for a significantly higher price than your original purchase price in a very short period of time (e.g. doubling your price in just 2-3 months), and your buyer happens to use the traditional bank financing, the lender will want to see some actual justification of such price hike in order to approve your house for financing. Your photos will then be used to prove the amount of effort and workmanship that you put into the renovation, which in turn justifies the higher price of the property.

Flashlight – Always bring a flashlight in case the power to the property hasn't been re-connected or isn't working. It would be a waste of your time and effort to go to your house but get no work done because there's no lighting.

Lockbox – Having a lockbox in the property with your house keys inside can save you significant time because, when needed, your contractors and employees still have access to the keys without you being on call or present. That can free up your time for multiple projects or deal hunting. After renovation is completed, remember to change the lockbox code to prevent theft.

Graph papers – A lot of houses you renovate probably don't require any major changes or redesign to the existing layouts. But if you do need to change the layouts, like tearing down some walls, adding windows or redesigning the bedroom, you'll need graph paper so that you can draw out your ideas properly along with corresponding measurements. That's why you should bring some graph paper, in case you need to make changes on the spot.

Step 2: Choosing A Contractor

For contractors to submit their bids for the jobs, you'll need to give them the scope or work so they know what work needs to be done and how to do pricing. You would also need to give them a standardized, itemized quote form so that the format of the bid looks the

same, which allows you to assess and compare the bid details a lot easier and quicker afterwards.

When you first advertise job availability for contractors to bid, let potential contractors know that you're not a retail customer, with multiple projects throughout the year, and you'll be accepting multiple bids on every job. That way you'll be able to receive highly competitive pricing on the bids. Before you start to pick a bid for a particular type of job, you would want to collect at least 3 bids for every type of contractor. Eventually, when you've worked with enough contractors with all the jobs you encounter, you'll build relationships with them and no longer need to get 3 quotes for every job you have in the future.

Beware that you don't accept from any contractor a flat quote for the entire job. You always want to see how each item of the job is priced. If you receive a significant discount on one element of the job, you can slide that contractor in for that specific part of the project, and you'll save yourself money. But without an itemized quote, you can't tell if a particular component of the job is priced too high, and you can't negotiate.

Step 3: Signing Paperwork

After you've reviewed all the bids and have decided on the ones that you want, you need to get paperwork signed so the project can start right away. Every contractor involved needs to agree, sign, and adhere to the terms and conditions of the contracts. Never start a project without finishing proper paperwork; otherwise, you won't have any protection against hidden troubles and

discrepancies down the road. Besides getting signatures at the meeting, you also need to clarify the method and frequency of communication and the timeline of the project tasks. Oftentimes, contractors want you to sign their version of paperwork. You must state clearly to them that you only do business with contractors who use your paperwork that lists prices, and your terms and conditions, so they're playing by your rules.

There are 5 important documents that need signatures before project initiation, including:

Independent contractor agreement – This is the most crucial document of all because it covers explicitly everything that is expected in the project, such as pricing, project schedule, late penalties, warranties, insurance, permit procurements, and contractors' conduct and behaviour. Never work with contractors who haven't signed this document.

Scope of work – After a full discussion and negotiation with the contractors, you need to finalize your scope of work so that both parties will agree and sign.

Payment schedule – This document sets up a timeline for payments based on level of work completion. Throughout the project, you'll set several benchmarks in which a portion of payment will be released once the benchmark has been reached. This document allows you to avoid problems/arguments during renovation, and to coordinate the schedules for payments and work at the same pace.

Contractor insurance/workers compensation form – This form requires the contractors to declare the minimum level of insurance they must have, and assigns them the responsibility of meeting that insurance. The insurance document should state who will be covered (note: your company needs to be one of the insured, not just their employees) and what will be covered (e.g. property in the project). Also, the insurance binder has to sign the document and to give you a copy of it.

Final lien waiver – This waiver is usually signed at the end of the renovation, but you need to get the paperwork ready and discuss with the contractors upfront just so they're aware of it. Basically, it protects you from any phony claims and lawsuits that the contractors file against your property at the end. Your contractors will need to sign it before they can receive the final payment.

Step 4: Managing Renovation

Before you start renovation, your contractors must show you all necessary permits, and coordinate all inspections required. Never compromise in obtaining permits because, after the project has started, any delay in obtaining permits will affect the renovation progress, and any work done without permits will make things illegal. Either way, your reputation as a reliable company/renovator and good relationships with building department officials will be undoubtedly damaged.

You should have a final meeting some time before the project initiates. Try to get as many contractors, sub-contractors or employees to come as possible, so that you can go over the scope of work, project benchmarks and communication expectation with everybody and answer any questions all in one shot. If there are any parties involved that don't know each other, this is the time to introduce them. After this meeting, work will begin, and you'll then focus on achieving benchmarks.

Remember to control and keep track of who goes in and out of the property and when during renovation.

Step 5: Checking And Closing Procedure

When the project is about to complete, walk around the house and check it against your scope of work. Before you release your final payment, make sure all work and touch-ups are completed, and the final lien waiver is signed off.

Step 6: Preparing For Sale

After all works are completed, you need to hire some cleaning workers to make the property look perfectly clean. If buyers see your house being all dusty and dirty with all the construction materials left behind, most likely they wouldn't be too pleased and would look at other houses instead. Remember, the first impression is crucial. Next, you need to stage your house, which is one of the best strategies for selling your house fast. Quite often, buyers have no idea how the space inside should be used when they first enter into an empty house. But when you stage your house properly, you help them imagine or visualize how it's like to live in the house, which in turn would facilitate their decision-making. Although you can stage the entire house, there are several key areas in the house that should be more focused: living room, kitchen, dining room, master bedroom, and master bathroom. Besides making the house look visually pleasing, you also want to make it olfactory appealing to people with the use of scented candles, air refresher, etc. Once staging is completed, you should definitely hire a professional photographer to take some good pictures of the property for marketing purposes. Professional photography is a good investment because quality pictures can bring out the vividness of the house, which leads to more viewings. You should also keep a copy of those photos for your work portfolio; having a professional portfolio can build your credibility and reputation as a quality renovator for your businesses in the future.

CHAPTER 13

WHOLESALING REAL ESTATE

You've come across a decent property, and after you've completed your due diligence, you believe it's a good purchase. But what if you don't have the time or money for it, or it isn't exactly the type of investment property that fits you? What should you do next? Simply let it go? Absolutely not! You can consider wholesaling it.

Wholesaling is either the sale of a purchase contract on a property to another investor (i.e. contract assignment), or the closing and immediate/quick sale of the property to another investor (i.e. double closing). This strategy is somewhat different from what we talked about before, which is to buy and renovate the property to turn it into a rental. One obvious advantage of wholesaling is the relatively short timeframe a deal can happen. With a property that requires renovation or redevelopment, you'll need more time to close a deal because it's more labour-intensive. But with wholesaling, sometimes you can realize profit from a deal in as fast as 6 weeks or less, starting from the moment you put a house under contract to the time you sell the contract to another investor. Of course, that depends on how you structure your purchase agreement with the homeowner or moving agreement with the tenant. If the property is vacant, a deal usually takes shorter time to complete.

The second advantage is that wholesaling involves less risk than other strategies like rental. It's true that all real estate investments, including wholesaling, have certain level of risks. However, with wholesaling, you'll have a great control of risk exposure when you know the intricacies of contract formation. That's why it's so important for you to be educated. You can also minimize your risk by limiting your deposit amount properly. We're not telling you to make a super small deposit like $50 or $100 for a $300,000 property. When the size of the deposit is too small, the seller may see you as having a lack of seriousness or sincerity in purchasing, and you may lose the deal. The size of deposit must seem appropriate; what I'm suggesting is a $500 deposit for all your deals. And if you have multiple offers with one seller simultaneously, you should then consider increasing your deposit to strengthen your intention to make a deal.

And since wholesaling takes a lot shorter time in general, it can minimize the market risk. Oftentimes, the housing market is largely affected by national trends or even global events. But it usually takes 6 months to a year for those impacts and repercussions to surface in the market. With wholesaling taking only a few weeks to months, you can reduce huge market fluctuations since the market changes very little in a short period of time.

Another great point about wholesaling is that it's a time efficient business. Compared with other investment methods, wholesaling doesn't take as much time and engagement from you. For example, you save significantly on the amount of time and effort by not having to arrange, supervise, and wait for various contractors to fix up a property. Most of the time, the wholesaling business involves logistics work, such as purchase negotiation, contract writing, paperwork processing, contract sale or double closing, and coordination of various parties in the transaction. This business is good for people who are busy with their regular day jobs and have limited personal time, as they can operate it on a part-time basis on the side.

A few things to keep in mind are that, within the contract, it's crucial for you put a clause that will give you the opportunity or permission to assign that contract to another purchaser. Otherwise, you can't sell the contract to others and wholesaling won't work. Also, the B.C provincial government recently announced its legal preparation to prohibit wholesaling, or "shadow flipping" as they call it, in order to curb the skyrocketing prices in its housing market. Hence, it is important to seek legal advice before you attempt the wholesale strategy.

THE WHOLESALING PROCESS

If you have never wholesaled real estate before, you may wonder what exactly wholesaling looks like. We'll break down the process in a series of steps. Keep in mind that some steps in wholesaling are the same as in other strategies.

Step 1: Looking For Deals

First, you need to create and execute marketing campaigns to let people – residents in your target area, or other investors – know that you're in business to buy properties. The process of "prospecting" is explained in a previous chapter.

Step 2: Analyzing Deals

Here, you analyze which properties have good potentials. In a previous chapter, we talked about how to analyze a deal in detail. A good way to evaluate a deal is to assess the property for the purpose of buying and renovating. If it makes business sense for you to buy and renovate a particular house, you know it's a good investment. Majority of investors who buy your contracts will evaluate the deal with renovation and/or rental in mind. So if you can find another investor to buy your contract, your analysis will serve him/her right. But if you can't find any buyers to take over the contract, at least you know you've got a good investment property that you can work on and potentially make a profit yourself. So you're not at a loss. Once you determine those houses have potentials, you will submit your offers to either the seller directly (FSBO) or the listing agents, which is step 3.

Step 3: Buying Contract Setup

In this step, you negotiate the sale price with the seller or listing agent. During your bargain, your price should have a big enough discount for two reasons. First, it has to make sense from the viewpoint of buying and renovating because, after closing, that's what you aim to do for yourself or other investors. Second, you leave enough profit margin for yourself so that when you sell the contract to other investors, you can still profit from the transaction. Once you agree on the sale price and terms, you'll then set up and sign the purchasing contract. In a previous chapter, we examined how to structure a deal and make an offer.

Step 4: Looking For Contract Buyer

After you get a contract, you now have the option of either closing the deal for yourself, or looking for potential buyers of the contract so you can earn a profit. When you're approaching your potential buyers, make absolutely sure you tell them clearly that you're just a "contract holder," not the property owner; legally, you don't own the house until you close on the property. Hence, all you have on hand for sale is a purchase and sale agreement, not the property or the title itself. When buyers express interest in buying the contract, you should do your due diligence to check them to ensure they're financially qualified for the deal.

Step 5: Closing Direction

If you have an interested buyer, you can close the contract by selling it to him/her or, you can double-close on the property.

Step 6: Closing Process

Lastly, you'll fulfill the closing process, which includes meeting all the deadlines, terms and conditions of the contract, and communicating with all parties involved throughout the process. Previously we have discussed about the things to watch out for during closing.

Wholesaling is a great strategy because it allows you to earn profits in a very short period of time. This comes especially helpful when you come across good deals but are too busy working with your day job or taking care of other renovating properties; you can still earn nice profits instead of letting opportunities pass.

CHAPTER 14

WHAT IS LEASE OPTION?

In real estate, you can have many different strategies other than the common way of buying and holding properties and the more creative wholesaling. Now let's look at another strategy that can generate quicker cash flows. It's called lease option, or "rent-to-own."

As the name suggests, lease option is a method in which the tenant can rent the property from you, with the option to purchase it from you at some time in the future (it's typically structured on a 3 to 5 year term). During this time, it gives you cash more quickly (or higher) than other strategies because it generates three sets of profits– deposit at the beginning, higher monthly cash flows (by a few hundred dollars per month), and a final payment at the end. This is called a "Purchase Lease Option." This method is good for those people who want to be home owners and have lots of liquid cash but have bad or even no credit histories to qualify for traditional mortgages from banks. You might raise a question of how someone can have cash but no credit. But believe me, they're a lot

more common in today's society than you think, especially in today's economic environment. They're in a situation where they don't qualify for a conventional mortgage, but financially they can afford one.

One example is the new immigrants to Canada. Often, they arrive here with their own savings from back home and/or have access to cash from overseas. Other than relying on their own assets, they also have strong determination to do whatever it takes to survive. Hence, financial resources and sustainability are not big issues for them. But since they haven't been in the country long enough, they have no credit history for a conventional mortgage approval from the banks. As a matter of fact, sometimes they might not even qualify for a credit card! It usually takes them about two to three years to build up that credit history before they can get a loan or mortgage. That's why our lease term of three to five years is good for them.

We also have those new graduates from professional programs in universities, such as dentistry, pharmacy, and medicine, etc. Those young professionals won't be approved for a mortgage right out of school because of the extreme debts they have in student loans. But since they have decent incomes at the start of their careers, they can afford to pay for a house mortgage, even after their regular payments for student loans.

Another group are people who make lots of money but with no credit history or are self-employed like independent contractors, and other people in the construction/renovation industry or other tradesmen. They can earn a lot of money – sometimes in form of cash – and they generally do not report it to the Canada Revenue Agency (which they should do, but that's beside the point). In their tax return, they can also legitimately expense a lot of their earnings, but that makes their taxable incomes too low to get a traditional mortgage. To get approved for a bank mortgage, they'll need three years to work up their income level and keep it consistent – another reason why our lease option is 3 to 5 year term.

However, not everyone is good for a lease option, and you must have a set of criteria in place to select the right kind of people to work with. The most importantly point is, you need to make sure your potential clients are financially stable and prudent. Let's say you have someone who filed bankruptcy before and has bad credit. Is he/she okay to work with? Well, you need to do some investigation or inquiry to find out the reason why. If they have stable jobs and/or know how to manage their finances, but went bankrupted due to marital breakup or something similar, that's still okay because you know the financial stability is there. But if the bankruptcy was due to poor money management, you can bet that they'll always have a hard time achieving financial stability since they have no knowledge and habits for financial health. Those are the people you don't want to work with. The only exception is, if they can come up with a huge amount of cash somehow, which can be used for deposit, then it will be okay as you won't be on the losing end; it's their responsibility to ensure they make the payments or the lease anyway.

Even if they haven't reached the stage of bankruptcy, you should still stay away from those who don't know how to manage their money and have ruined their credit scores. Remember, the bottom line is, financial stability and prudence is crucial to the success of this venture. At the end of the day, you're in this business to achieve a win-win situation for everyone. So do those unfit candidates exist? Sure they do! They are not difficult to find – like big money spenders whose expenses are usually greater than incomes, or they constantly max-out their credit cards but with just minimum payment every month.

SETTING UP LEASE OPTION

Now that you've learned what a lease option is and who can be a suitable candidate. How do you set one up?

There are two different scenarios to consider here. The first scenario is, if you already own a property and want to put a rent-to-own tenant in place. The second is where you allow your potential rent-to-own clients go out and find a property they like, and then you purchase it and set them up in a lease option with that new property.

The overall process is pretty much the same for both scenarios in that you first start advertising the program as much as possible and as many ways as possible such as, through friends, current/potential tenants, buyer's lists, newspaper ads and online (e.g. Facebook, Kijiji). When people contact you and express their interest in the program, you'll get them to fill out an application, either physically or electronically. You'll then assess the information on their applications. In the case rent of existing tenants, you'll see if they qualify for the house they're currently living in. For other prospects who are suitable for a lease option, you'll contact them and explain to them the purpose and details of

the program more thoroughly. When they agree to participate, you'll inform them the maximum value of a property they can qualify for (e.g. $300,000) based on the financial information they provided. They will then go out and look at one or a few properties they like. If they happen to bring you a few properties but can't decide which one, you'll pick one for them. Afterwards, your clients and your realtor will go see the house together, and if they all like it, you'll make an offer to buy it on behalf of your clients. Once the deal is closed, you'll become the property owner, and your clients will become the tenants of your house, with the option to buy it from you in three to 5 years' time.

STREAMS OF CASH FLOW IN LEASE OPTION

Remember the beauty of a lease option is getting you quicker cash in 3 different ways? Let's take a look at each of them using our $300,000 property example.

Deposit / Down Payment At The Beginning

At the beginning, when you create the lease option, you'll ask your client for at least a 5% deposit (so you're not at the losing end if the deal does not conclude with a sale). In this case, you'll get a deposit of at least $15,000, in which you'll potentially have to return at the end of lease term. However, if your client doesn't have the deposit amount in cash because it is your deal, you may consider taking something else of value instead as the deposit. Let us say they offer you something valuable as collateral, like a painting or an antique car, then you really have to judge its value and see if it's a fair substitute. But this will become tricky because most of us aren't experts in assessing arts and antiques. Hence, at the end of the day, cash is still preferred. Another thing to keep in mind is that it doesn't really matter where the down payment comes from or how your clients get it. They might borrow it from family, friends, or whoever, but it doesn't concern you; ultimately, you're not responsible for paying their lenders back. And as much as you want to make sure their money is legal, sometimes you really have no way of telling/tracing, so you just have to assume it's okay.

We mentioned that this deposit will potentially be given back to the tenants at the end of the term. I say "potentially" because, in reality, you don't really need to physically return it to them. Here is why: at the end of the term, if your client decides to exercise the option, your lawyer can deduct the deposit amount from tenant's purchase price for the property. Financially, it doesn't make a difference whether you return the $15,000 deposit to the tenants and charge them the full amount on the property, or you keep the deposit and credit them with a sale price that is reduced by the deposit. You can do it either way, but keeping the deposit and crediting your clients has less hassle.

On the other hand, if your clients fail to fulfill their monthly commitments, they will lose the $15,000 deposit. If they decide not to buy the property and walk away after three or five years, you'll get to keep the deposit as well (plus monthly credits, which will be explained next). Hence, once you receive the deposit, you can treat it as non-refundable and spend it.

Monthly Rent Throughout The Term

The second source of quicker (or higher) cash flow is the monthly rent. Let's say the current monthly rent in the market is $1,500 for this particular style of property. You'll charge your tenants a rent of $1,900 per month, in which you will credit the extra monthly $400 towards their final purchase price at the end of the lease option term when they exercise the option to buy. (The credit amount is negotiable with the clients; if they only want $300 per month towards the final purchase, the monthly rent would become $1,800, and so on.) If they decide not to buy then you'll get to keep the extra $400 a month as profit. Plus, let's assume your monthly expenses, including mortgage payment and amortized insurance and property tax, is $1,200. With the market rent, you're already profiting $300 per month. So, in total, the monthly profit in your pocket is now $700 from the lease option, which is higher than simply renting.

Final Payment At The End

When you first set up the final purchase price for the lease option, you have to account for home value appreciation. Let's assume an annual 5% appreciation for the next three years. After doing the calculation, you realize that you can sell your $300,000 house for $347,288.50 after three years (or round it to $347,000 to make thing easy). So if your clients are qualified for a conventional mortgage and want to buy this house in three years, they'll have to pay $347,000. Therefore, you'll set the final purchase price at $347,000, with the clients knowing about and agreeing with the spread. What your clients don't realize is how much you pay for that house at present time. Throughout this book, we've been talking about looking for deals, which means we never pay for the asking prices. Let's say you buy the house today at 10% below market value at $270,000, instead of $300,000. So at the end of the 3-year term, you've got a potential profit of $77,000 (= $30,000 + $47,000) from the sale of your house.

That is a good profit but you have to remember that you have already realized some of that profit during the term of the lease option. You took $15,000 as a deposit at the start of the term, and you have been receiving $400 a month during the term. So at the time of purchase the lawyer will credit the purchasers with $29,400 towards the purchase price of $347,000 and you will then only get $47,600 (= $77,000 − $29,400) at the closing. Still nothing to sneeze at!

There is an added benefit to the purchasers as well. They need to get a mortgage from the bank to purchase the property, and in most cases they would be getting a 90% mortgage and have to come up with 10% or $34,700 as their down payment. But they already have $29,400 as a purchase credit which means they only have to come up with $5,300 additional cash for their full down payment. So in reality it is much easier for them to purchase using the lease option method.

Put It Together

One thing to keep in mind is, when your client can't fulfill their monthly commitment or they decide to forfeit their option to buy, you don't return their deposit or monthly credits. When you first set up your lease option agreement, you're in business to help your client through the time they can't get a mortgage while you get a profit from the arrangement. If they fail to commit in the process or walk away at the end and you pay them back their money, you're simply acting like a rental without any further obligation on them, which is not what you're in business for with the lease option.

So if the deal fails and falls apart after 2 years, you'll keep the deposit of $15,000 and the total credit of $9,600 (= $400 x 24 months) from the monthly rent – that's $24,600 in total profit! You can then finish the deal by either selling your house with a $24,600 discount on the sale price, or turning around and finding another client to do another "rent-to-own" option. You can even just rent it out like a regular buy-and-hold property if you're happy with the $24,600 profit and think the lease option is too much trouble for you. The choice is yours.

THE SANDWICH LEASE OPTION

There is a second type of Lease Option and it is called the "Sandwich Lease Option." It's pretty complicated because, essentially, it contains two lease options in one package – you first rent a house from a homeowner with the option to buy it from him/her, and then you turn around and rent it to another party with the option to buy it from you. As you can see, things can get messy with three parties involved, so it isn't recommended for novice investors.

CHAPTER 15

COMMERCIAL REAL ESTATE

Now we're going to look at a small subsection of real estate investing, in particular, commercial real estate. Commercial real estate is basically anything bigger than a couple of single-family units.

There are many reasons to move up into commercial real estate investing. One of the main reasons for considering a commercial property is that they are generally far more expensive than single residential units so you can place a lot more capital at once, and in return, you get a much larger cash flow. What we mean is that one commercial property may be equivalent to 10 smaller residential Properties.

One major advantage of investing in commercial properties is the ease of determining the current market value of a commercial property. With residential properties, the market value of an individual property is determined for the most part by its comparables. However, for commercial property, the main determining factor in its valuation is the cash flow that is generated from the property itself. So, in simplistic terms, a commercial property that generates twice as much the cash flow as another one will be valued at twice as much the value as the other one. This makes it very easy to increase the value of your property; all you have to do is to increase its cash flow. When you increase the rent from the tenants in your property, you are effectively increasing the value of the property.

Another major reason for commercial properties is that it is actually easier to finance a commercial property than a residential property. This may sound counter-intuitive when you first hear it, but it is actually true. When banks and lending institutions consider financing a commercial property, the single factor that they are looking at is the steady cash flow that is coming from that property. They look at how steady and how consistent those cash flows are. The financial background of the person applying for the loan does not really come into play that much. So in reality, it is the property that determines whether or not the bank will give out a mortgage. With residential property, it is exactly the opposite. The bank is more concerned with the person applying for the loan than the revenue that the property generates. The bank will want to make sure that the person applying for the loan can afford the mortgage payments, even if the property does not generate any income.

There are generally two types of commercial properties: residential or multi-family properties, and non-residential properties.

NON RESIDENTIAL PROPERTIES

There are three major types of non-residential properties. They are retail, offices, and industrial. There are many advantages to non-residential commercial properties, and one of the major advantages is that you are dealing with businesses rather than individuals. Generally, businesses act in a much more logical fashion than individuals. Also, businesses tend to be a lot more financially stable than individuals and, hence, easier to deal with.

With commercial properties, you are also dealing with what we call triple net leases. A triple net lease means that the owner of the property receives a net rental amount, and the tenant is responsible for all the other expenses, such as utilities, property taxes, insurance, repairs, maintenance, etc.

Another advantage is that the leases tend to last for much longer terms. Commercial leases can run anywhere from 5, 10 to 15 years, with extensions as well. Your cash flow is then guaranteed for that extended period of time. The banks really like to see this when they are financing a commercial property. Also, the leases will probably have some form of escalation clause as part of their terms. That means that, at certain times during the lease, the rent will automatically increase. Since the value of a commercial property is determined by the rent it generates when the rents escalate, your property value will also increase at the same time.

Property Management on commercial property is also much easier. Since the tenants are generally responsible for all the repairs and maintenance of the property, those are something you generally do not have to worry about. Also, most commercial leases have a management fee built into them that the tenant has to pay for. So if you like you can just hire a management company to look after the property for you and have the tenant pay for it.

RESIDENTIAL COMMERCIAL PROPERTIES

Residential commercial property is made up of multi-family properties that can be anything from a fourplex up to a 100 unit apartment building or even larger complexes.

The main benefit of multi-family commercial projects is that all your rental units are centrally located in one area, and not spread out all over the city or even all over the county. Since all of your units are centralized, you can also have centralized property management, with an on-site manager inside the complex to look after the daily operations of the complex. You can also have on-site maintenance people to handle the day-to-day routine maintenance and repairs required for such a project. Effectively, the economics of scale work in your favour with a multi-family commercial project.

Multi-family commercial projects or apartment buildings are some of our favourite forms of investments. Due to the larger dollar amounts involved with these types of projects, they are also the projects where we take in the higher net worth investors. Since we like to have only a few investors in each individual project, we generally take a larger amount of capital from each investor when we place them in a commercial project. To be considered for such project, we generally like to see at least a $250,000 investment from an individual. However, we still always have smaller single-family units investments, in which smaller investors can participate.

ABOUT THE AUTHORS

PATRICK NG

Patrick has 4 different university education in Canada: Bachelor of Pharmacy, Bachelor of Commerce (Finance), Bachelor of Arts (Drama and Foreign Language), and MBA (International Business).

Originally born in the international financial city of Hong Kong, he has always been interested in finance and real estate investment, and hasn't stopped learning ever since. He began his career in the pharmacy profession, but later took a career change and focused on his own investment and consulting business. In addition to his experience in investment management, during his education in Bachelor of Commerce after-degree and subsequent MBA degree, he enriched his body of knowledge in investment by taking real estate investment courses, and participating in various workshops on how to invest and raise capital for real estate. With a passion to help others succeed, he gave out educational presentations, and later teamed up with his fellow MBA alumnus, Larry Yakiwczuk, to develop this book so they can help educate more people with their wealth of knowledge.

LARRY YAKIWCZUK

Larry Yakiwczuk is the founder and owner of the Buckaru Group of Companies. He has 6 University Degrees, 30 years of real-estate investing experience, 15 years' experience trading derivatives, and has been financially free for the past 15 years. His proprietary investing strategies allow his investors to achieve significant returns on a consistent basis, regardless of the current market conditions. His mission is to educate the small investor and help them achieve their own financial goals!

Larry started his real estate investing career in the early 1980's while he was still in his twenties and attending University. He has extensive experience in all aspects of real estate investing including various forms of residential rental real estate as well as various forms of commercial real estate, including warehousing and industrial complexes.

Recently he's been concentrating more on investment placement and management for his real estate investors. He concentrates on projects that will give his investors significant and consistent returns regardless of the current market conditions.

His experience in the single-family residential area began as most people's experience begins, that's with small houses and condos. He started out by buying individual housing units. He also started with some small Condominiums as well. He concentrated on all aspects of managing those properties including finding new tenants, property management, and eventually reselling the properties when the market was higher than it was when he bought them. At one point he started to specialize in small rental Condominiums. He found a great deal on the MLS that was listed by a realtor that specialized in this area. After he bought the first unit from this realtor, they struck a bond together, and since then, whenever that Realtor had a unit that fulfilled Larry's criteria, the agent would call Larry directly rather than listing the unit for sale to the public. The realtor knew that after he gave Larry the pertinent information he would have a yes or no answer on that same phone call. This resulted in Larry obtaining 10 Condominiums within the same high rise condo complex, and resulted in Larry owning approximately 15% of the entire complex. He then sat as president on the condo board and was able to effectively control the whole complex.

Larry also was able to obtain bank foreclosures directly from the bank because of the good banking relationships that he had established. An example of this is a 15 unit condominium complex that he obtained from the bank as a result of a foreclosure. He was actually able to get the foreclosing bank to fund his purchase of the property. He managed that property for a number of years, and finally resold the units individually for a substantial profit. He also has experience with purchase, management, and sale of small apartment buildings as well. He started off with small 8 and 15 unit apartment buildings that were actually not in his local area but were located in small residential communities around the Edmonton area. This gave him extensive training in dealing with long-distance management of commercial residential properties.

Larry has extensive experience in the area of true commercial properties such as warehousing and Industrial complexes. With these types of properties, he was able to gain experience in commercial leasing and negotiation techniques. He has experience in this type of commercial properties, both as an investor and as an end user. He currently owns a number of commercial warehouse buildings that are being used for his auction company business as well as other businesses.

In one case, he purchased a warehouse property for use in his auction business; however, he quickly realized that the property would generate more cash flow by being rented out to a local trucking company. A couple of years later, he sold that property to a competing trucking company for a significant profit.

Larry is now more concerned about investment management, and purchasing properties and managing them for his investors. He specializes in two forms of investor participation in his projects. The type of investor participation in his real estate projects is determined by the needs of the investor.

If an investor is concerned mostly with cash flow from his investments, then a mortgage investment is the investment of choice. This type of investment will give Larry's investors consistent cash flow over extended periods of time regardless of what is happening in the markets and is not dependent on a property being sold any time in the future. This type of investment is particularly suited to investors that need to live of the cash flow from their investments, such as retirement funds. Whether it is retirement funds are straight cash, Larry always has mortgages available to place investor funds.

The second form of investment Larry participates in with his investors is in the form of equity or a joint venture partnership. In this type of investment, the investor is actually part owner of the property. In this case, there is generally no cash flow to the investor during the time of the investment however the investor does participate in the equity appreciation of the property and sees significant returns when the property is eventually sold. This type of investment is more suited to the younger investor, or the investor that simply wants to park his capital for a period of time and is not dependant on the cash flow from the investment. The returns on this type of investment are generally higher than the mortgage investments, but take longer to realize.

Because of his vast experience in the real estate and investment industries, Larry is always willing to talk to anybody about investing in real estate. If you have available cash and are ready to make an investment, please contact him directly.

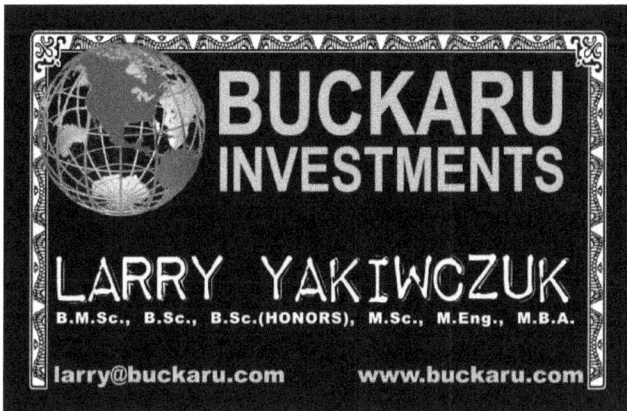

6 Bonuses

5 Homes to Financial Freedom   FREE
A webinar recording explaining how you can achieve financial freedom with the equivalent cash flow of 80 rentals from owning just 5 homes. (Value of $49.99)
Visit **www.MagicMirrorInvesting.com/book**

Making
FREE
A webinar ventures and with very Visit

Real Money With Joint Ventures
recording discussing the specifics about joint how they can be a short cut to vast residual profits little initial work. (Value of $49.99)
www.MagicMirrorInvesting.com/book

Rent To Own with No Money and No Risk   FREE
A webinar recording with over 60 minutes on rent to own secrets and different ways to increase your profits and minimize risks in real estate investing. (Value of $49.99)
Visit **www.MagicMirrorInvesting.com/book**

A Millionaire's Mindset   FREE
A webinar recording giving you an insight into the mindset of a millionaire where you will learn a bit about business, real estate, and the stock market. (Value of $49.99)
Visit **www.MagicMirrorInvesting.com/book**

Power Investing   FREE
A webinar recording giving you an insight into the mindset of a Millionaire where you will learn a bit about the stock market and investing. (Value of $49.99)
Visit **www.MagicMirrorInvesting.com/book**